Everyone has a st
story. In his book, *Co*
But God, Wayne Heil has shared an interesting narrative that begins with a German family moving to Russia, escaping by night to America in fear of the oncoming Bolshevik revolution, and finding a home in South Dakota. It was here that Wayne's personal story begins in Mobridge. What follows is a fascinating narrative of loving families, beautiful romance, marriage to two beautiful women, varied successful ministries, and sometimes even bitter disappointment.

In spite of several setbacks and discouragement, this story is about a triumphant life that is rooted in the rich soil of a deep faith. The church would be blessed if more people of faith would share their trials and triumphs as honestly as Wayne Heil has in this engaging account of his faith journey.

—Donald S. Aultman
Retired Minister and Educator

I first met Wayne Heil in the summer of 1978 during a brief intermission of the business sessions of the Church of God General Assembly. I was only twenty-seven years of age, serving as the state youth and Christian education director of Kansas and was preparing to move my precious family to Oklahoma. Even though our limited visit only allowed us a short span of time to talk, Wayne Heil took that time to get acquainted with a young preacher and to let him know how important it was for the overseer to get to know him.

Over the years, our paths have crossed frequently and Wayne has never changed. He has always been the gracious, gentle Christian shepherd, always wanting to help others. For the past four years, we have grown much closer. I see him and Sister Ruby frequently at Garden Plaza because every day he sits with my father during the dinner hour. It was Wayne Heil who convinced my dad to move there, and he has been a wonderful friend to us all.

While reading his book, *Complexities Along My Life's Journey—But God*, I laughed and wept. What a wonderful story that is so beautifully written. It is a must-read for all, and I commend it highly to everyone who needs to know that God is always there!

—Donnie W. Smith, D.Min.
Executive Administrator
Church of God Division of Care

The life of Wayne Heil became intertwined with my life on the last day of 1953 when he arrived in Haiti. Because of his extensive experience as a builder and contractor, he was appointed as overseer of Haiti with the understanding that he would also build three missionary residences and a new facility for the Bible School. Those three years made an invaluable contribution to the Church of God in Haiti, and that campus continues to be a consecrated place of ministry.

I am grateful to my friend and brother, Wayne Heil, for writing the story of his life and ministry. It contains so much of God faithfulness; so much for the reader to learn and to enjoy. I commend my friend and his book.

—James M. Beaty, Ph.D

I have known Wayne Heil as a colleague in ministry for nearly three decades, but Myrlene and I came to be close friends when he became a part of the church we pastored (Loxley Church of God) in Alabama. Not only are we friends, but we were also privileged to observe the late-in-life courtship and subsequently to participate in the marriage of Wayne and Ruby Heil.

For seven years I was Ruby's pastor, and for most of that, Wayne's pastor as well. It was also my distinct honor, after their marriage, to employ them as members of our pastoral staff, with Wayne and Ruby serving as a team in the role of senior adult pastors. Myrlene and I enjoyed many great meals, challenging table board games, and exciting trips with the Heils!

It has been said that, "Every man has a story to tell." Wayne Heil's story is more than just "Wayne's Story." It is the story of Wayne, Virgie, Ruby, and even of Ruby's late husband, James L. Slay. It is the story of Wayne's son and Ruby's sons. It is the story of ministry and of business, success and disappointment, victory, and then defeat replaced by victory.

It is my privilege to not only have lived part of this story, but to personally know the principle characters within!

—Dr. James E. Cossey,
Administrative Coordinator
USA Missions
Church of God International Offices
Cleveland, Tennessee

Complexities Along My Life's Journey— But God

Wayne Heil

Scripture passages are taken from
the King James Version of the Holy Bible.

ISBN: 978-1-59684-729-3

2012 © Copyrights by WH Publications
All Rights Reserved
Printed by Derek Press
Cleveland, Tennessee

This book can be purchased at the following sites.
Amazon.com (Paperback)
Amazon Kindle eBook
Google eBook

You may contact the author at wwheil@hotmail.com

CONTENTS

Dedication	9
Acknowledgments	11
Foreword	13
Introduction	15
1 A Brand New Venture–But God	21
2 Life's Connections	31
3 My Beginning and What I Thought	37
4 My! How Things Changed	47
5 Houston	53
6 Bible Training School	61
7 Back to Texas	71
8 Back to School	79
9 Wow	87
10 Tremont Avenue–Greenville, South Carolina	95
11 Missions	103
12 Grand Avenue	117
13 Extreme Circumstances	131
14 Back North	145
15 Evangelism	155

16	*Hawaii*	163
17	*Military Missions*	179
18	*State Overseer Assignment*	191
19	*Looking Back*	199
20	*Compounding Problems*	209
21	*Transitions*	219
22	*A New Problem*	225
23	*Legal Review*	231
24	*Destiny Adjustments*	237
25	*Single– Now What?*	249
26	*I Married My Sweetheart*	259
27	*My Future at Loxley*	267
28	*Moving Again*	283
29	*Health Problems*	287
30	*Special Times*	293
31	*Life's Complexities–My Synopsis*	299

DEDICATION

By writing this series of word pictures, I indicate how my life followed a very exciting path on the road to my destiny. I dedicate this book to my only living son, C. Duane Heil, to the memory of Virgie (Ainsworth) Heil, my spouse of fifty-plus years, to my current spouse of over seventeen years, Ruby (Slay) Heil, and also to the memory of my mom and dad, Thelma and Henry Heil.

Time establishes beginnings and endings. Though the dates and persons spoken of on these pages are relevant to perhaps only my family, they are memories I recall. As wonderful and unique as family memories are to me, I dedicate to past and present relatives, my heritage. I thank God for them.

ACKNOWLEDGMENTS

In every activity there is recognition of those who help to make a project complete. More than one person enters into the planning and the action to complete any function. When I began my writing, I was dependent upon many people to help me complete my project. If this whole plot were a jig-saw puzzle, it would take dozens of pieces of varied sizes to make the picture complete. I started the plot of my life's story with a vision and a revelation. Life to me has been a fabulous venture through the maze of excitement, conflict, problems, solutions, decisions, and conclusions of how I made my journey. Now I come to the end of this writing with a story that needs to be shared.

I am thankful for the support I received from friends who encouraged me to complete this work. Special credit is given to Ruby, my wife, for her help in keeping the content of my story in a fluid style.

I am indebted to Wanda Griffith who edited all the script and made certain that I was presenting my data in good writing style, by keeping the story plot simple, readable, and understandable. When I would be too verbose, she would help me by simplifying the terminology and state the story-plot in understandable language. Thank you again and again.

I am pleased to list the names of those special friends who have supported me with their endorsements. To Dr. Donnie Smith, executive administrator, Division of Care Ministries; Dr. Donald S. Aultman, retired director of education Ministries, Dr. James Cossey, administrative coordinator, USA Missions, and Dr. James M. Beaty, retired missionary and educator.

I am especially indebted to Clyne Buxton, longtime personal friend and colleague, for writing the foreword to this story. We have shared similar experiences. Clyne has been a great encouragement to me in completing this work.

These are very special friends with whom I have shared a close friendship for decades. To have them express support to me makes me very grateful and thankful to each of them.

FOREWORD

This is indeed a splendid account. It is exceptionally well written, candid, and detailed. Once you begin to read it, you will have difficulty putting it down. It is intense, intricate, and parts of it read like a mystery novel.

Wayne Heil is indeed a prodigious person. I am so glad that he has given us a straight-forward, clear, detailed document of his journey. You will be awe-stricken as you find the many things God has accomplished through him.

Who else do you know who has had a myriad of achievements and did them all with excellence? To learn of his many successes during his illustrious lifetime is mind-boggling and nearly unbelievable. Here are some of his attainments: guitarist, accordionist, singer, builder, accountant, pastor, missionary, director of evangelism, state overseer, and servicemen's director.

I have had the privilege of knowing Wayne for many years. First at a distance, such as at church conventions, but then later we pastored close together in South Alabama. We got to know each other better as we had fellowship, including some golf.

I was always moved by Wayne Heil's speeches at the Church of God General Assembly. His resonant, clear-speaking voice was captivating. More importantly was his poignant, keen intellect. Whatever the subject under discussion, we all could count on Wayne being lucid, reasonable, and logical.

As you travel with Wayne on his journey, you will find him to be a man of integrity, even in turbulent, stressful situations. John MacDonald commented: "*Integrity* is not a conditional word. It does not blow in the wind or change with the weather. It is your inner image of yourself, and if you look there and see a man who won't cheat, then you know he never will." When I read that recently, I thought of my friend Wayne.

Also, he has an abiding appreciation for the Bible, which he reads, memorizes, and preaches. For example, when he reached the hospital where his wife, Virgie, was gravely ill, his first words to her was to quote an encouraging verse from the Psalms.

God's Word is eminent in Wayne's life. Coleridge said, "Never yet did there exist a full faith in the divine Word which did not expand the intellect while it purified the heart; which did not multiply the aims and objects of the understanding while it fixed and simplified those of the desires and passions."

Wayne Heil is a man of faith, a man of integrity, and a man fully committed to God's Holy Word. The world needs many more men like that.

—Clyne W. Buxton

INTRODUCTION

To title an autobiography with a strange name, and then create a book from it to be read by whoever seems intrigued by its title, may seem out of the ordinary. Yet, it is my intent to be candid. I must also be factual. Sometimes the facts will be dramatic and sometime the issues that become facts will be hurtful. In spite of judgment, actual or implied, it will be my best intent to define every issue or situation as they are in my life's history. Therefore, this book will contain complex and maybe complicated descriptions of certain issues. Webster's definition of the word *complex* also has a synonym—"intricate, involved, tangled or knotty." With these conditions, I title my autobiography *Complexities Along My Life's Journey—But God*.

It is not easy to take the multitude of episodes that have, to date, made complete the story of 87 years of my life. Sometimes the pictures I paint with words seem to be fuzzy. At other times they are dramatic; sometimes they are catastrophic, and sometimes just plain ordinary expressions. Painting my life's pictures in words reflects not only my thinking about when something out of the ordinary happened, but also wondering what I did about the crisis, or question why the incident occurred.

In 1976, in Hawaii, I pinpoint a very important drama in my life to show how God came into my life's picture. While the beginning of the episode appeared to be a simple dream or vision, the magnitude of the events that unfolded are perhaps too dramatic to analyze. But God who foreknows everything and who gave to man the ability to think, decide, and listen showed me that I am dependent on God to help me under every circumstance.

With my memory *I recall*, with my mind *I wonder*; and with my logic, *I question.* The experiences of the biblical character Joseph in Genesis 30-50 depict the story of his life. From the good to the bad, the events that revealed thirteen years of his life's complexities were stated emphatically by Joseph to his brothers. As Joseph said in Genesis 50:19-20, "Fear not: for am I in the place of God? But as for you, ye thought evil against me, but God meant it unto good, to bring to pass, as it is this day, to save much people alive."

When I write about the experiences of my life and expand the subject with the preposition *but*, I am generally contrasting the issues of the subject matter. When my subject is referred to with a concept of a positive and also a negative condition, I begin to question . . . why? When God is found to be in the solution or conclusion, I recognize that the omniscient God is aware of every aspect of my life.

In grammar school I learned the use of words in grammatical structure. Sentences are modified with the use of the conjunction to expand upon the enlarging of the content of the subject and the predicate. The use of the conjunction *and* infers a condition of increase. The use of the conjunction *but* infers a condition of an alternate, either positively or negatively.

As an example of these conditions I will express the emphasis. "I will sing." The enlarging of the meaning to the next sentence shows. "I will sing *and* play the piano." By contrast, the conjunction *but* often expresses an opposite meaning. "I will sing, *but* I will not play the piano." The conjunction *but* often implies a negative alternative. However, it may also be emphatic in the positive. "I thought; I questioned; I wondered; *but* God made the difference in the conclusion. Here, the positive emphasis prevails.

I will give you an overview of episodes that have occurred in my life. I declare to you that whether I wondered, thought, or questioned about them, my God has allowed me to have some wonderful experiences. I have noticed some dramatic factors that have opened my eyes about which I will address in other chapters.

Someone said, "Life is but a dream." As I look back in the rearview mirror of my life, I have had some bad experiences I wish were only dreams! "Life is a reality" with its valleys, its mountaintops, and its plateaus. I will express my feelings, my moods, and my experiences and the reason I express "life as a reality." If and when I refer to the conclusion that the "But God" condition applies, I can understand how my life's experiences have helped in many ways.

Many of my experiences have been of such wonderful magnitude. I often try to explain them verbally by using terms that help me explain the ecstasy or the agony of that experience. To express it another way, I use the description of being on the mountaintop or walking through a valley.

Let me remind you, there is a mountaintop only when it is associated to the valley that establishes its base. To have two mountaintops adjoining each other, there must be a valley between them. This helps me to remember the experiences I have had. I often have rejoiced about the high and lofty feeling that has followed the rich experiences associated with my spiritual attitude. I am also aware of the despondent feeling related to some of the circumstances that brought me to the valley of despair. Yes, there have been times that people have handed me a "double whammy"; but God has always known me, helped me, inspired me, and through the Word of God, I often have found the road through the wilderness, out of the valley, and into the opposite extreme of my despondent mood. It is then that I found myself on the high plateau of life.

The financial status of today's economy sometimes affects the budget's balance. Conditions relating to the economic collapse of financial institutions adversely affect retirement funds. This is why I say the ups and downs of life are often described as a very hilly adventure of life.

Some issues and conditions unraveled with associates that made me wonder whether the path I follow can or will lead me, in the end, to the status of happiness. But God has helped me, guided me, encouraged me, and directed me.

My early life experiences were framed with the special scripture taught me by my Bible School teacher, Avis Swiger, when I was a student in Bible Training School (B.T. S.) seventy years ago in Sevierville, Tennessee. Proverbs 3:5-6 says, "Trust in the Lord with all thine heart, and lean not unto thine own understanding. In all thy ways acknowledge Him and He shall direct thy paths,"

In my later life, I have wondered where the path of life was taking me. I have intertwined my philosophy of what have been my experiences to Romans 8:28: "And we know that all things work together for good to them that love God, to them who are the called according to his purpose." While the scripture does not say that all things that we encounter are always good; but the results will be for good. In other words, whether we perceive the experience as good or bad, everything works together for good. When I "wonder if" or question "why," my life has been affected with the good, the bad, and the ugly, I am reminded that my God knows it all. He will show me; He will teach me; and He will help me.

At times I wondered where God was in my experiences, as they seemed to have such a negative position when I thought things should turn out differently. At other times, I recognized that my God had not forsaken me in my crisis.

During those times in life, I have been excited when my option has been the *"But God"* factor. I define the last sentence in this way: "I learned that God is definitely a part of my life's functions and activity."

—Wayne Heil

CHAPTER 1

A BRAND-NEW VENTURE— BUT GOD

"My flesh and my heart faileth, But God is the strength of my heart and my portion forever" (Psalm 73:26).

Life's complexities are in every era of life. This event of my story is placed out of chronological order in this book. By starting with this story, I hope to explain the purpose for my book title and help you understand the way life unfolded for me. However, it is placed here so that you may begin to know the magnitude of what happened in the middle years of my life. I was fifty years old when these events happened.

A New Assignment

I was notified by Dr. Cecil B. Knight in June 1974 that it was not possible for me to be transferred to another state in the position of evangelism director. In those years, each state wanted its own minister to hold that position. I was three years as pastor at Ferndale and five years as Michigan's first state evangelism director. I fulfilled eight wonderful years in Michigan. However, there would be a new assignment given me if I would accept it.

The Church of God officials assigned me as the servicemen's director to the Far East at the 1974 General Assembly. My new assignment would start in August, and I was to live in Hawaii, work with all the military bases there, and also have all the bases in the Far East as my responsibility. It was a different ministry than I had been accustomed to for the thirty-two years I had been preaching. I had not been in the war zones of the world, because I had a draft exemption as a preacher during World War II. Now I was to work with all military bases in the Pacific and Asia. Every base in Hawaii was operating at full capacity because of the Vietnam War.

When the position of my ministry to the military was identified, Dr. Knight discussed the location of my activities and the type of work I would be doing. I was to work with the military, and my residence was to be in Hawaii. I was about to enter the threshold of a brand-new venture at a wonderful venue, Hawaii. Dr. Knight informed me of the magnitude of this assignment. I was excited to accept the challenge of this new venture. Dr. Knight continued to inform me of a problem that needed some attention in Thailand. My assignment there would be to try to work out the difficulties.

Travel to the countries of Asia was budgeted from the International Offices, since all of the work was military-related. The first two travel years in my military assignment were rigidly controlled because of the limited financial budget. I didn't have funds to allow Virgie to travel with me. This situation was supposed to change at the next General Assembly by granting me a sufficient budget.

My schedule to the Orient was to make my visits and convocation dates every four months. Each trip was 16 to 20-thousand miles from home and would last four to six weeks. Consequently, I was in Hawaii to work with the local military bases for a two- to three-month period before going to the Orient.

When I made my introductory contacts with the chaplain's office at Pearl Harbor, I was informed it would be impossible for me to fit this schedule into my first trip. The reason was defined at length. America was still in war with North Vietnam. Thailand was the area where American war planes landed after finishing their mission in Vietnam. However, the chaplain said to me, "I think I can work it out where you can get there. I am the command chaplain of the Pacific. If you will work under me, I will get clearance for you."

In six weeks I was called to the chaplain's office at Pearl Harbor. I had received clearance and 24 sets of orders to be used as my introduction to each base commander in any country where we had U. S. military bases. I was shocked to learn of my status. Washington military authority had given me clearance to travel anywhere and also given me a GS-16-E Rank. Not knowing what that meant, I began to ask. The chaplain said, "You have been given the Civil Service rank equal to a One Star General. You will outrank every chaplain in your area of duty. When you arrive, you will be escorted to the base commander's office. From there, you will minister on any base that is open to religious services."

Pomp and Dignity

The next shock I had was looking at the name on my documents. My name was spelled *Wayne **Hell***. Since my schedule of travel was immediate, there was not time to have Washington reissue new orders. At every stop and base, my apologies about the wrong spelling drew much laughter. My assignments and destinations to bases in Japan, Korea, Okinawa, Philippines, and Taiwan were filled with pomp and dignity.

When I arrived in Guam, the lieutenant general said in stern comment, "I'm glad your first name isn't "Raisin," or you wouldn't be welcome on my base." After another good laugh, we got down to business. My destination was the Udon Airbase in Thailand. Travel from Bangkok to the base was by military aircraft, since civilian aircraft was not allowed to take me there. The base command officers were there to greet the plane. The base commander informed all in attendance that a general and a colonel and eighteen other servicemen were on the plane. The chaplain said to the commander, "He ain't no general; he's a preacher." My assignment authorized by Dr. Knight was one of investigation, which I completed with dignity. The result was the Udon chaplain was transferred.

The first two years of my assignment were exciting! I was working with the military and conducting convocations at the different bases that welcomed our ministry, via chaplaincy polity.

At the end of my second year in Hawaii, an extraordinary event took place that affected my activity and upset my actions. The budget money for Virgie's travel was not appropriated.

Here the story gets complex. As I stated in the first paragraph of my introductory remarks, the complexities of my life became very intricate and knotty.

By pinpointing these very unusual circumstances, I begin with a vision and finalize with complexities and a decision that I did not make. But God made the difference in the conclusion. The unfolding of life and the possibility of death became a nightmare in our existence.

The Doctors' Reports

My reason for sharing this drama at this particular time is to show how my God, knowing the future, helped me to better accept the crisis I would face five months later. Virgie, my lovely wife, became a companion to me when I was seventeen. She was ten months older than I. Never in my wildest dreams did I perceive that she could be anything but healthy. At five-foot seven and weighing 105 pounds, her appearance was, to me, of a beautiful and gorgeous woman. Thirteen months after we married, Duane was born. In a follow-up medical review from her physician, Virgie and I were given a report that devastated us. Doctors informed us that sometime in her teen years, Virgie had contracted some kind of a virus that ultimately damaged her heart. Virgie had never shown any effects of a physical deficiency before receiving the doctors' reports. Now the circumstances unfolded with a twist that we did not wish to accept or believe. The mitral valve in her heart was severely malfunctioning. Instead of receiving the blood from her artery in its full-force flow, that valve was damaged and the blood was leaking back from whence it came. While this report was validated with a secondary check-up; the results were the same and the reports were unchanged.

The doctors informed us that because of this damaged valve, Virgie would be compelled to undergo surgery for its repair. Also devastating was the alternative condition if she chose not to have the surgery. Virgie was told that if she did not submit to surgery, she would die before she would see her forty-fifth birthday.

The law of life and death has somehow been projected as an automatic law from the book of God—the Bible.

Normal life has been evaluated by experts who seem to predict life's average lifespan. To start planning for long life and to calculate one's destiny by the terms set by insurance underwriters may often become a broken dream. The norm of the underwriters says we will get old; and God's Word praises those who reach three-score and ten years, but nothing guarantees this.

The result of Virgie's heart valve problems caused the death of three premature infants before she reached the age of thirty-three. Virgie did everything that was expected of a minister's spouse and she was my companion. All of her activities and duties brought her to that devastating period when everything went into a tailspin.

Open-Heart Surgery

In 1966 the collapse came. The doctors had said, "You must have surgery before age forty-five or you will die." Now at age forty-two, the doctors described the conditions in the following way: "It is not a matter of when you submit to surgery . . . but where!"

We moved to Maryland to pastor a wonderful congregation in the lovely city of Salisbury. We could go to one of the famous hospitals nearby, but because we were originally from Houston and all our kinfolk were there, we went to Houston. Dr. Michael DeBakey, a world-renowned heart surgeon in Houston, accepted our local doctor's reports and surgery was scheduled. The success of that event was marred by a contaminated blood transfusion. Virgie underwent a severe reaction for two years after her surgery from the hepatitis she got from the bad blood. Two years later, the artificial valve that had been installed in her heart was damaged due to breaking of sutures within the heart. Open-heart surgery for the second time was mandatory to repair the broken sutures that held the valve in the internal portion of her heart. The surgery was successful and life for us returned to normal.

As stated earlier, we moved to Hawaii in 1974. The church officials assigned me as the servicemen's director to the Far East at the 1974 General Assembly. Dr. Cecil Knight informed me of the magnitude of this assignment. I was excited to accept the challenge of this new venture. Because this was a new appointment with no parsonage, we rented a residence in Aiea.

One year later money from the sale of our home in Michigan became available and we bought a condo in Mililani Town, Hawaii. Frequently, we would walk to McDonalds for a snack. This became a regular routine.

My Vision

Here the events get complex. One morning in the summer of 1976, just before I woke up from sleep, I saw at the top of the wall of my bedroom two words: **BUT GOD.** I was startled. I did not know the reason for this revelation or why it should be shown to me in that manner. When I went to my office that morning, I began a research. *Strong's Concordance* revealed dozens of scriptures. Of special interest was Psalm 73:26: "My flesh and my heart faileth: **But God** (my emphasis) is the strength of my heart, and my portion forever."

I have always been a believer in what we normally call "God's will." I have not always known the meaning of those words. Yet, I always had a response and reaction to every event of my experiences as being ordered by God.

The issues revealed in the vision that early morning were ultimately to show me that God foreknew the issues that would unfold five months later. I thought that my research of the Bible to locate all the scriptures relating to the "**but God**" theme was a marvelous revelation that I had not known before. Now I perceive that God, who foreknows everything, was showing me how His divine will was unfolding. The next five paragraphs reveal those events. The marvelous circumstance of this event was tied to the budget. If the travel budget had been appropriated in August of 1976, Virgie would have been with me in Korea at the time of her collapse. There would not have been any hospital or doctor to provide for her. Being in Dallas, she was instantly in the care of a doctor who knew exactly how to perform the surgery and preserve her life. My desires were for Virgie to be my companion on my trips to Asia, but God designed the alternative plan that was to follow.

Little did I know then how God would bring to pass the events of the next five months. On each trip to McDonalds, Virgie told me how difficult her health conditions were. Her constant statement was, "I would rather die than go through surgery again."

Again, the complexity of circumstances begins the unraveling of our thread of life. As stated earlier in this chapter, the travel budget did not provide for both of us to go to Asia. In early October, the overseer of Alaska, Reverend Bill Rayburn invited Virgie and me to speak at a fall convention in Anchorage, Alaska, with all expenses paid. We felt spiritually invigorated by this and enjoyed our time with the Rayburns.

After the close of the convention, I headed west toward Korea and Virgie traveled southeast to Dallas to spend the next five weeks with her sister, Edna.

Edna and Elbert Mitchell owned a health-food business there. One morning Virgie collapsed in her sister's store. That collapse was just like Edna had seen in a dream five months earlier. At that time, Edna had called Hawaii and asked about her sister, Virgie, but she did not explain the reason for her inquiry. Virgie was transported by ambulance to a local Dallas hospital. The issues were diagnosed and reported to Edna. Virgie was told that she must either have surgery or she would die. I was still in Korea. At midnight I called Dallas. It was 8 a.m. in Dallas when I spoke with her brother, Bill Ainsworth, who was standing by Virgie's bed, and he quoted to me Psalm 73:26.

The trip from Korea to Dallas was long. After entering Virgie's hospital room and greeting her, I listened to her doctor as he told me about Virgie's prognosis. Virgie interrupted the conversation in a challenging sort of way to say, "Dr. DeBakey was my surgeon before. Doctor, what are your credentials?" After learning the status of the Dallas surgeon, Virgie had a complete turn in her decision, whereas months before, she had said, "I would rather die than go through surgery again."

She said, "Doctor, when you operate, I want my old valve back. The artificial valve had been in her heart for ten years. But now she changed her mind. Her faith had been restored. She quoted again the verse she had heard me identify in my vision five months earlier—Psalm 73:26: "My flesh and my heart faileth, but God is the strength of my heart and my portion forever."

Her surgery was a success. Virgie was convinced that by having surgery, the future for her would be good. The surgeon gave to Virgie the valve that had been in her heart for ten years. This event, though complex to interpret at its beginning, became the drama upon which my past and my future continues to unfold. I know beyond the shadow of a doubt that God gave me two words in my vision that brought to me the scripture in Psalm 73:26 that gave us peace in our hearts during our crisis. The pattern of all of my experiences from that day forward has been reflected on how God has been (past), is (present), and will be (future) in all of the events and situations I have and will encounter.

Life's complexities bring to me unusual events that are not always good. Sometime I think everything is a failure, but then I check all the facts and find that God has helped me through every one and it is okay. I often think life should be different, *but God* knows how to help me and the end result is dramatically different and sometimes very exciting.

CHAPTER 2

LIFE'S CONNECTION

"In the beginning, God. . . . ."
(Genesis 1:1).

In my introduction, I declared, *"for me life is a reality."* This is my autobiography. Most of the time, I will be recalling memories. Also, I will interweave the issues of my life with the history that made my life as it was and now is.

Mom's Writings

Much of the information in this chapter is taken from my mom's genealogy reports I received from her in 1977.

The beginning has to do with an era before I was born, where my relatives came from, their lifestyle, and how they become a part of my life, which will help to reveal my life's story. According to Mom's information, in the early part of the nineteenth century, a colony of Germans who had lived near Berlin, Germany, made a decision to leave that particular area because it was beginning to become thickly settled. Many of the families migrated to near Kiev, Russia. The Krein family, Dad's mother's family, settled near Neidorf, Russia, and the Heils near the neighboring town of Gliecksdahl, Russia. There in 1857, Jacob L. Heil, my grandfather, was born October 24, to Ludwig and Louisa Heil. Dorothea Krein, my grandmother, was born July 4, 1861. Jacob Heil and Dorothea Krein were married February 8, 1881.

Jacob Heil, my grandfather, told my mom that Ludwig, my great-grandfather, had acquired quite a bit of land when they went to Russia in 1853. When my grandfather, Jacob Heil, married Dorothea and they began to have a family, Jacob acquired his father's land and worked it on a large scale. Many young Russians and Jews were hired to help him work the land.

After living in that area about fifteen years, something happened that caused things to change. One day one of the Jewish workers whom Jacob trusted went to my grandfather with some information that he would reveal only after Jacob was sworn to secrecy. That young Jewish farm worker told him the Russian Government was planning to turn Bolshevik and advised my grandfather to take his family and leave secretly from Russia.

He told him if he stayed, the Bolsheviks would take everything he had and would threaten death to all foreigners living there. Under cover of darkness, Jacob and Dorothea, my grandparents, took their children and a hired girl, and with only their personal belongings, escaped across the Russian border.

In May 1893 the Heil family left Russia and migrated to the United States. Their ultimate destination brought them to South Dakota. Dorothea bore eleven children to Jacob; seven were born in Russia and four in South Dakota. Henry, my father, the seventh son of Jacob and Dorothea Heil, was born near Avon, South Dakota, on November 16, 1895. All of the family moved to the northern part of the state in the early part of the twentieth century and settled near Loyalton, South Dakota. In 1907 Jacob Heil sold that farm and moved to Mobridge, a new settlement on the Missouri River.

A new railroad was being built from Aberdeen westward. When materials were shipped, they were addressed to the "Missouri bridge." The words *Missouri Bridge* were finally abbreviated so the address read "Mo. Bridge." That seemed a good name for a town, so the people in the new town who were mostly crewmen on the bridge construction gang decided Mobridge was the best name for the new railroad town. More and more people built homes since they planned to stay in the area and work on the new railroad terminal. As young men, Louie and Johnny, Dad's brothers, got jobs too. Even Henry, my dad, did odd jobs for a short while. The new four-room house Dad's father built was the second house in the town. There were lots of tents for temporary living quarters in warm weather, but those who planned to stay, built houses for permanent homes. They needed a place of recreation, so my grandfather built a pool hall and bowling alley. As there were so many boys in the Heil family, they didn't need to hire any help. August, Dad's brother, was manager of the pool hall and the younger boys learned to play pool and bowl. While the Jacob Heil family owned and ran the pool hall and bowling alley, it seemed only natural for Henry, my dad, to spend a lot of his time at the establishment. He became very proficient in playing pool and very few men in town could win if he was one of the players.

Again, I will quote from my mother's personal letters.

"Sixty- six days sailing the Atlantic in 1832 finally brought the Fougeron family to the United States from Belfort, France. They settled in Buffalo, New York. Simon Jacob Fougeron, my mother's grandfather, married Marie Marshall, the Buffalo mayor's daughter.

The Fougerons were well known in Buffalo, New York, because of the marriage relationship to the city mayor. Two streets in Buffalo were named for Mom's family. Two generations later, the Fougeron family became a known part of my family history."

George Henry Fougeron Jr., born March 13, 1876, was my grandfather. Ellen Bessie Riddle, born January 3, 1882, was my grandmother. They married on January 8, 1902, near Crete, Nebraska. They lived in the same area until 1913 when they moved to Minnesota. George and Ellen had a family of nine children—four sons and five daughters. Thelma, my mom, was the second child, born in Dorchester, Nebraska, February 23, 1904.

I have used my mother's family letters to define the Fougeron history. My mother's parents, George and Ellen Fougeron, moved to Minnesota in the early part of the twentieth century. Their parents migrated to America in the mid-nineteenth century and settled in Buffalo, New York. The family migration led them to Nebraska and ultimately to Minnesota.

In 1923 my father, Henry, went to Minnesota to learn the carpenter trade from his older brother. In order to establish the details of how Dad and Mom found each other, I will cite the references from Mom's letters: Henry lived with his brother, August, and learned the building trade rapidly as he liked that kind of work. His younger brother, Ed, who went with him and as a young helper, learned the building trade also. They were glad to be together again and to be able to work together. After only one year as an apprentice, Henry decided to make it on his own. August tried to discourage this as Henry was a good worker. Henry was determined to be a successful builder. He started his first jobs promising satisfactory jobs or no money. He always had work from then on. During the winters of 1922 and 1923, he worked on a road-building gang. It was bitter cold and he often worked double shifts because workers were hard to get, but that wasn't too bad because it meant a larger check. Then in the spring, he did some remodeling and repair work in Morris, Minnesota. From there, he went to Alberta, Minnesota, eight miles away, to build a house, and he also did a large repair job on the roof of the schoolhouse.

One day as Henry worked on the new house, Thelma went down to take a picture of her father, George Fougeron and her brothers, who were pouring cement for the septic tank. One of her brothers introduced her to Henry. After Henry met Thelma that day, he just couldn't keep his mind on his work too well. When he laid his hammer down to cut a board, he couldn't find it when he needed it, even though it was on the saw-horse or right under his feet. When he went to the lumberyard to order material, he always looked across the street to see if Thelma might be at the window, and often she was. The truth of the matter was they were both "love sick."

In 1922, Thelma, my mom, went to normal school to become certified as a rural school teacher. She was responsible for making the fire in the pot-belly stove on cold days, cleaning the floors, and teaching all eight grades each day. There were thirty-five students in all of her classes. She was paid the enormous salary of $100 per month. To say the least, Thelma was not interested in staying in the teaching profession very long. Her teaching role lasted only one year.

Mom and Dad got married in Minnesota on December 27, 1923. *This ends the history part of where and when. What happened next?*

CHAPTER 3

MY BEGINNING AND WHAT I THOUGHT

"God ... breathed into his nostril the breath of life" (Genesis 2:7)

One cold winter morning in Sioux City Iowa, Henry and Thelma Heil received their first 'bundle of joy'—ME. That was November 15, 1924. My weight was eight pounds. They named me Wayne Warren. Since I was not named after Grandpas, or Uncles, I guess they just picked my name out of a hat. I came from a large family. My mother, Thelma Heil, gave birth to ten children, of whom I was the first. At one year of age, my parents moved to Mobridge, South Dakota. Dad was asked to come there by his parents. They provided my family a lot at the edge of this small town. The construction of a bridge across the Missouri River created the location of this small town in north-central South Dakota. When the bridge was completed, the name became *Mobridge*. The town began to grow. That was in the first decade of the twentieth century. Dad was a contractor and he tried to keep the family happy by providing us with a good living quarters. Oh yes, when the ten children made our family complete, Dad taught the nine boys to become builders. Our sister had to fit into this kind of picture the best way she could.

Grandpa Heil wanted my father to help him in the construction business. My first memories were of going to Grandpa's house and getting a great big portion of sauerkraut from his great big fifty-five gallon crock-pot. Grandpa would cut the cabbage, put in the right amount of vinegar and other seasonings, and cover the huge crock. He would leave it for weeks until it fermented and became German Sauerkraut. I remember eating it when I was just a three-year-old kid. I still like it today.

Life in my first few years was normal. Nothing extra special happened that I remember. I was aware that our family increased by four more siblings (all boys) before I reached six years of age. I don't remember much about those first few years because I didn't get the attention that I had received before the other "four bundles" arrived. I guess I became challenged for number-one rank. Even though we lived in nice houses Dad built, sometimes we lived in them as they were being built. I have to say there was some fun in that. Dad was always building for somebody else to earn his living and provide for his family's needs. At the same time, he was always striving to complete an unfinished house for his own growing family. The first things I really remembered were the dust storms and the tumble weeds that collected at Grandpa Heil's fence at the east side of town.

In 1977, my mom wrote her life story, *Reminiscing over the Years*. In it, she told about Dad and me and the event that started me on a career of becoming a builder. Little did I know then that becoming a master builder and contractor would be a related function in my ministry. Having been a master builder, as well as a minister, was an asset in my church assignments.

This next paragraph, taken from Mom's writing, tells how it all started.

> Henry had lots of work after we moved to Mobridge. After he finished his folk's home, he started work for Mr. A. H. Brown, the city millionaire who owned at least half the town. Every fall Mr. Brown went to Palm Beach, Florida, where he owned the biggest part of that town. He was good to Henry though and soon realized that he was a competent foreman. Whenever Mr. Brown had a big building to put up, he merely told Henry to start work. The summer Wayne was four and a half years old, Wayne asked his daddy one day if he could go to work. At first I refused, but Henry said, "Yes, let him go," so Wayne went to work. He immediately asked for a nail apron and a hammer. When Henry tied the apron on Wayne, he put two hands full of nails in the apron, thinking Wayne would have nails to play with for at least two weeks. Wayne wanted to help build, so Henry put him with two of his helpers putting on sub flooring. In two hours, Wayne was back asking his daddy for more nails. By 5 p.m. Wayne had used all his nails in the subfloor and the helpers got quite a charge out of his efforts. Every night Henry had me put time down for all the men and on weekends it was turned in for the paychecks. That week at the bottom of the page I wrote, "Four hours for Wayne Heil at 10 cents per hour." When the secretary read the timesheet to Mr. Brown, he asked, 'What's that ... what's that?' Henry said, "My wife put that in for a joke." Mr. Brown's son spoke up and said, "Dad, that's right; I saw Wayne working all afternoon," so Mr. Brown said, "Write him a check for

forty cents." I don't think Wayne ever got a larger check in his life that made him feel as important as that one did. I had to help him sign his name at the grocery store, and he got four dimes that went into his bank as soon as he got home. I remember that event as though it were last year."

My Early Years

My next experiences had to do when I entered the first grade. Mobridge was a small town. I entered a school to find students who were not friendly to each class member. I had my good and bad days. I had my fights, because the kids at school called me "Rusty Iron Face," because of the freckles all over my face. I didn't like to be insulted or to be called insulting names by anybody. I grew up to be defensive. My friends were few and limited because of my embarrassment over my freckles.

However, life for me changed. The depression years began after the crash of 1929. Becoming a Christian at the age of nine in 1934, I found my life in Christ one of excitement. As a young boy, during the depression years of the '30s, I had little. My family lost their possessions after the 1929 crash and we became a poor family. During that time period, many people were poor.

When Reverend Paul H. Walker brought the message of Christ to our town of Mobridge, South Dakota, in February of 1934, little did I realize then the impact that the revival and the and subsequent events would have on my life. Mom and Dad were converted in that revival and received a transforming work of God on their lives. Instead of remaining staunch German Lutheran in belief and church-practice, my folks allied with this jubilant group of over 100 believers who found God in the Pentecostal revival conducted by the Paul H. Walker Evangelistic Party. One of my first remembrances of that meeting was observing a little five-year-old boy, the evangelist's son, in that series of services. Paul Laverne Walker was a part of that evangelistic party who would later become the general overseer of the Church of God.

My Salvation Experience

My personal experience in Christ came that summer of 1934 when I found Christ as my Savior in a tent revival at Grand Crossing Boulevard and First Avenue East in Mobridge. I listened to the Evangelist Reverend David C. Boatwright bring a challenging message that convicted me. As a nine-year-old barefoot boy, I knelt in the sawdust at a plank bench altar and found Jesus as my Savior.

Memories of my first camp meeting in the Church of God was in Minot, North Dakota, in 1935. There were no cabins, no motels, so we camped for the whole period—yes ten days—in a tent. Mom brought lots of canned goods for us to eat. I remember while my parents were in one service that I got a large can of pork and beans and ate the whole thing. To say the least, I never chose pork and beans as my choice food thereafter.

My First Camp Meeting

I was intrigued by the camp meeting services. I remember getting a glimpse of General Overseer S. W. Latimer when I was ten years old. I have had the wonderful occasion and distinction of identifying with, knowing, meeting, or working with every general overseer in the Church of God but two: A. J. Tomlinson and F. J. Lee. This does not make me an historian of these times as it might relate to the various relationships with these leaders, but it does permit me the option of defining certain issues as I have encountered or perceived them.

My spiritual life was affected by every service I attended as a young boy. I became involved in each service, made friends, and enjoyed my new lifestyle. I was no longer introverted. I had a better self-image. I was only eleven years old, but God forever changed me at the Bible School service in Lemon, South Dakota, in 1936. While there, I felt that I received a call from God to preach the Gospel. Though God's calling was upon me, it took six years before I saw the door opening for me to fulfill that call. I was in the sixth grade of school, and because of my conversion, I was now also being labeled as a "Holy Roller"—a slanderous term against new Pentecostals of that era. This made me quite reactionary. I asked my parents to let me quit school when I finished the eighth grade because of this. I thought that because I had the call to preach, my parents would send me to Bible School in Tennessee. They would have if they could, but being poor, they could not provide the funds.

The Great Depression Years

This decade was known as the Great Depression; jobs were scarce and pay was poor. I remember the reports that men worked on the WPA—government-provided jobs that paid $1 per day. People searched for employment wherever they could find it. This time in the lives of all our family was the point of utter poverty. No one had food for the table. We were not alone. Everybody suffered during the Great Depression. I remember taking my little red wagon and going to the train station to wait for the government food to come in. When the train arrived, everyone picked up sacks of moldy flour, lard, and whatever else was distributed at that time. I also remember that Mom would take the cloth cotton sacks and get to work on her sewing machine. The end result would become underclothes for us boys and clothes for my newborn sister. This kind of life did not end at the end of a summer. It continued throughout the 1930s—the Depression Years. Although President Roosevelt changed the course of political action with the establishment of the "New Deal," things continued in their bleak process. Everybody struggled to survive.

Cooking for Dad

I quote further from Mom's diary:

In September of 1938, Henry heard of a government project that was to build a couple of schoolhouses for teachers near Belvedere, South Dakota. We made a trip to Minneapolis, Minnesota, to sign the contract, on the way leaving the children with Grandma Fougeron in Minnesota.

This location was a government project located on one of the reservations in southern South Dakota, about 200 miles south of Mobridge. As Wayne had finished the eighth grade, he stayed out of school that fall and went to Belvedere to be the cook on the job. Henry took a tent and camping equipment and they stayed on the job site.

I was going to become the best cook I could be for Dad, Grandpa Fougeron, and Uncle Floyd Fougeron. As a thirteen year old, I learned that living in a tent with winter snow and only a pot-belly stove for staying warm wasn't ideal living. With only a fairly small stove, it seemed I could only get warm one side at a time.

I didn't have anybody to play with because no youngsters were on the project. I found one of the guys on the job who had a Harley Davidson Motorcycle. The opportunity was given me to ride that "two-wheeler" into Belvedere The distance was eight miles south of the project location. There were no paved roads, only gravel. As a thirteen year old, I received instructions and took off. The wind was strong and the road was clear. At eighty miles an hour, I got my first and last thrill of being a motorcyclist. I don't remember if I promised God I wouldn't ride another motorcycle, but I should have. I did not realize the danger I had put myself in until it was over. I then realized how stupid I was to do that. But now I find 80 miles per hour in a car is a nice speed.

Quicksand

At the project was a lake where Uncle Floyd and I decided one day to take a walk. About three quarters of the way around, we came to a little marshy place from the creek that fed the lake. I was walking behind as the path was narrow. All of a sudden, my uncle instantly sank up to his waist in that marshy ground. He screamed and told me not to go any further. Fortunately, when he bent over to catch a strong tree in front of him, he was able to pull himself out of that quicksand area. Things could have been different, **But God** knew the present and the future. He allowed my uncle and me a greater future.

The job was finished before winter was over and jobs were still very scarce. Mom had two brothers, Harold and William, who lived in Houston, Texas. They wrote her and said that anyone who wanted to work could find a job. This event became a venture of huge proportions! When I think back on my life's beginning, I wonder what would my life have been if my parents had not seen a vision of something better down South. If I had stayed in that small north central town in South Dakota, what might my story have been?

We moved.

CHAPTER 4

MY HOW THINGS CHANGED!

*"As for man, his days are as grass,
as a flower of the field, so he flourisheth"*
(Psalm 103:15).

Memory is an essential element in everything that I shall write and have written. In my introduction I identify three references upon which I pinpoint these word pictures. With memory recall it becomes obvious that "I Wonder." When I wondered how the present and then its future might become, my mind sometimes was foggy. I must say it often was in a state of uncertainty. Many things, however, are as "clear as a bell." As I remember the past, eighty years ago, I recall, I wonder, but then comes my future. I write on...

The depression years of the 1930s were a time of severe drought in South Dakota and most of the mid-central part of the United States. In fact, one year Walworth County, where we lived, was declared the driest county in the nation. I was aware of these conditions when the clouds in the sky seemed to indicate a pending rain. However, instead of rain, the wind would blow and the dust storm that followed would leave a heavy blanket of black dust at every windowsill in our house. We didn't have the kind of controlled window frames that would keep out the dust that came with this kind of storm.

In those days I remember well the tumbleweeds that would accumulate at the wire fences that designated a person's property line. The yards were always covered with weeds. When the sandstorms came, the tumbleweeds rolled, and if nothing became a barrier, the tumbleweeds accumulated at the next fence. I grew up not knowing that, if well maintained, yards could be beautiful.

A Whipping to Remember

We moved to the west side of town when Dad became a general contractor. According to Mom, he built a beautiful seven-room house and bath, a full basement, and space enough in the attic to complete two large bedrooms in the future. It was completed just as any house should be and which any buyer would expect and accept. This new house was within one block of the railroad tracks. The one thing I remember specifically was an order from my Mom: "Don't ever cross the train tracks or you will be given a whipping." One day someone told Mom that I had done the forbidden. Heretofore, my spankings had always been a mild spat on my bottom. This one was very different. Mom said, "No, it will not be me; it will be your dad who will give you the whipping."

When Dad came home, he did just exactly what Mom said. I will not go into detail except to say it was not, and I repeat, not just a mild spat on the bottom. That was the first and last time I ever had so severe a punishment from my dad. Things around the house at that time were always about normal. We four little boys got along quite well. Our life seemed to follow a routine. Dad would play pool in the evenings, usually after the good supper that Mom fixed. One of Mom's rules was, "Clean your plate," which we always followed religiously. Then came the 1929 Financial Crash!

My fourth brother, Alton Carroll, was born January 29, 1930. Because he was fat at birth, Mom called him her *little fat pumpkin*. As he grew up, it was shortened to *Punky*. But after he joined the Air Force, he told everyone that his name was just plain *Punk*.

We were now a family of five boys, Wayne, (no nick name) Deryl (Tex), L.E. (Bud), Darvel (Dodo), and A. C. (Punk). The five years and two months since my birthday were meager years of existence due to the economic conditions.

Financially, things got worse for our family in 1931. Dad could no longer make the mortgage payments on our nice new home. A local doctor in town offered Dad two lots and material to build another home for the equity of our home on Fourth Avenue West in Mobridge. Sadly enough in two years, that next house also belonged to Dr. Twining.

Three 'Hobos'

Dad rented a house and we moved across town into a large old two-story house with a coal furnace in the basement. It had deteriorated with age. Three of Dad's nephews came that fall to visit us. Because the house was large and they had a place to eat and sleep, they decided to make an extended stay.

In those days, the common term for folks who went from place to place doing nothing was *hobos*. Because coal was so expensive, Dad took these three hobos two miles to the river and cut down trees. No, we didn't have chain saws in those days. We used the old fashioned cross-cut saw. Two men cut with the big cross cut, while the other two split the wood, loaded it into the truck, and hauled it home. That's how we all kept warm. Finally, the hobos decided to leave our house and head back toward home in California, riding on the underside of a railroad boxcar, which was the standard travel method in those days for hobos.

That next year 1934 was the year my next brother came to our family. He was named *Jerome Henry*. He inherited the nickname *Gebo* because he didn't want to be called by the two long names when everybody else had a short name. In 1935 my only sister, Wanda, was born. Though Mom had wanted the firstborn to be a girl, she was the seventh child who filled her life with the frills and beauty she wanted for her family. In 1937, baby number eight came to be a part of our growing family. His name was Arlen Dean. In his teen years, his school comrades nicknamed him *Fitty*. Even though it was a highly unusual name, Dean never reacted negatively. With Mom and Dad, we were now a family of ten.

Texas Bound

My story continues with how we survived. Finding employment anywhere was difficult. Jobs were scarce and a long way from home. Then came a call from two of Mom's brothers. Her brothers informed my dad that work could be found in Texas by anyone who wanted a job. With that news, we soon began the chore of packing. Dad built a trailer to handle our household belongings. I remember the trailer was made of a wooden frame over the two-wheel metal axel. Dad put a waterproof canvas over the trailer to keep its contents dry.

We left Mobridge in the dead of winter, March 3, 1939. Driving with a loaded trailer, Mom's diary told of Dad driving thirty miles per hour with that loaded trailer. Our car was a 1936 two-door Chevrolet Sedan. Dad had bought his new car in 1936 when a special government pension for his service in World War I was received. In those days an inexpensive car like Dad's was not the size of the luxury vehicles of that day. It was quite a bit smaller with four in the front seat. Dad was at the wheel and Mom at his right with the two babies between them. The front seat of that 1936 Chevy was long and not divided. Six boys occupied the backseat. When restroom stops were necessary, all ten of us unloaded from that car. With the necessary "pit stops," flat tires, and repairs, it made our days slow and very long.

This trip meant traveling a zigzag course, since we had to go from South Dakota to Minnesota to say our goodbyes to grandparents. Then on to Nebraska, to the place where Mom grew up as a child. We arrived at 2 o'clock in the morning. Looking back, I wonder how happy they were to see ten people at that hour. We spent the balance of that night with a cousin near Lincoln. From there we traveled through Kansas and Oklahoma. Our speed efficiency was affected continually as flat tires became our problems. In those days tires were repaired by the occupants while on the road with patches and air pumps. My brother Deryl (Tex) and I, always helped Dad during our seven days of travel to Texas.

On the sixth day after leaving Mobridge, according to Mom, Dad made the decision to get to Houston before stopping again. We left Oklahoma City at 8:30 a.m. By 6 p.m. we were four miles north of Streetman going 40 miles per hour. As we crested a small hill, the rear tire on the car blew out and Dad lost control of the car. We were "plum" scared. The trailer overturned in the middle of the highway. Passers-by stopped and helped reload the trailer with the salvaged furniture. We had no choice; we had to spend the night in Streetman.

The next morning Dad arranged to get a tire and spare inner-tube. Since his money was about gone, he persuaded the salesman at the station to loan him $35 to pay for the purchases. For this, he gave the man at the station his Elgin watch as collateral, with the promise that he would repay him in one month, which he did.

We arrived at Bill Fougeron's house in Houston, Texas, at 4 p.m., Friday, March 10, 1939. I thought we had arrived in Heaven . . . there were flowers and green grass everywhere!

Moving from the North to the South did not enter my mind as being a part of how my life would be affected in the future years. But God who foreknows everything, would teach me that life in Houston would have a dramatic emphasis in how He would help me.

CHAPTER 5

HOUSTON

*"But speaking the truth in love,
may grow up. . . ."* (Ephesians 4:15).

As we came into the city of Houston, Texas, that Friday, March 10, 1939, I saw the sign giving the size of the city—292,000—City of Houston. One week earlier we had left a town of less than 5,000 people. I felt as though I could get lost in a hurry in such a large place, but since I had finished the eighth grade and my favorite subject in school was geography, I was convinced that I could find my way around town. All I needed was a map and the opportunity !

Our family stayed with my Uncle Bill and Aunt Jo for ten days. Mom said Dad found a house in the Heights on the west side of Houston on 27th street. Only after the rent was paid, the landlord asked if there were children. Mom said, "We thought he was going to back out when we said eight, but he didn't."

A Shack, a Garage, and a Chicken Coop

One month later, two large lots were obtained on King Street in North Houston. We were four miles from the courthouse and almost out in the country. One lot had a one-room, unfinished shack that was 12 x 18 feet with a one-car garage and a lean-to chicken coop. Six boys had beds in the garage next to the chickens. This was home for six months. Competition with the chickens became a real problem. The crowing of the rooster was a constant pain in the neck. The second lot was to be used to build our new home

After we arrived in Houston, Dad found work and he never slowed down. I became his full-time helper. With a family of ten mouths to feed, it was necessary that I help in order to keep food on the table. Each week I would give my paycheck to Mom to help the family. I kept $5 a week as my spending money.

The first week after our arrival in Houston, we located the only Church of God that was located in the Heights, a section in the northwest area of the city. We had moved to our first rented home less than two miles from the church. It was exciting to get into worship at our new location on Alston Street. Pastor E. M. Smith (nicknamed *Red* for his carrot-red hair), was a very cordial and likable pastor. We moved from the northwest side of town to the northeast side on King Street five weeks after arriving in Houston. The Houston church was a small congregation;. Being a family of ten, we made a good addition for the congregation size at our new church.

Becoming A Top-Rate Craftsman

As was stated earlier, Dad went to work immediately. Building new houses seemed to be a very good venture. I remember the price of the first home Dad built for the lumber-yard owner. The 1939 price for that home was $3,500—yes $3,500. Of course it was still during the Depression decade and also just before World War II.

During that three-year time period—March 1939 until March 1942—a small fourteen-year old boy named *Wayne* had matured into a husky seventeen-year-old man. My father taught me the tricks of the trade and I learned to be a top-rate craftsman. One of the first lessons I learned was how to saw a straight line. Another lesson I learned was how to measure the board to be the right length when it was to be sawed. I will never forget the instruction given me when Dad told me, "I cut the board twice, and it was still too short." I learned quickly what Dad meant when he said, "Don't cut a board too short, because it is thereafter only a piece of scrap wood."

The first year our family was in Texas seemed exciting. The economy was picking up because the world was beginning to show concern about the European activity between Germany and its neighbors. Hitler had started his move to overtake or conquer them; war was eminent.

War Clouds

Houston began to expand because of labor demands for making ships to transport the goods created by the pending war stimulus. The Japanese were moving south with armies to determine their position to gain oil for their country.

The United States was aware that war clouds were prevalent, both in Europe and in Asia. At that time the United States did not have men fighting on the battlefield. The United States policy began by manufacturing needed war supplies. Whether manufacturing airplanes, ships, tanks, or any other items used in wars, the labor market boomed and so did the economy. Wages more than doubled in a year. Our local church congregation grew due to labor demands. There were openings for any male who wanted to work. At that time we had a change in pastors.

The Pastor's Daughter

In October 1941, Reverend W. F. Ainsworth came to Houston from a pastoral position in New Orleans. In his family were three girls and two boys. Being involved in my church, I was happy to see a new group of worshipers. One who caught my eye immediately was a seventeen-year-old beauty, a daughter of the new pastor. Her name was *Virginia Mae. Virgie* became her new name soon after meeting her. She was five feet, seven in height. She had a lovely figure and weighed 105 pounds. Every time I walked into church, I looked to see if she had arrived.

Since the church congregation was small, the members considered it essential to have the parsonage under the same roof as the sanctuary. The small parsonage was in the back section of the building. On each side of the church entrance doors were two small Sunday school rooms. The two sons of the pastor slept in one of these rooms and vacated it when it was time for a worship service. The other five members—the pastor, his wife and three daughters—were in cramped quarters for their sleep time. The exit from the parsonage was out of the rear of the building.

At this point in my life I began to wonder about what my possible options my future held. I was a strong-minded person and thought I knew what I wanted life to be. I was also physically quite strong, since I had been a full-time hard worker with my dad for five years. I began to think that now I was old enough, strong enough, and mentally sound enough to think about a companion.

Every time the church doors opened, I was there early. I soon convinced Virgie that I was interested in dating. Since her parents were protective of their oldest daughter, I was not allowed to have many dates. About the only time Virgie was allowed to be with me was after church. It was less than two blocks to the nearest ice cream store where nearly everybody went after church. Virgie and

I made good use of this time even though I would have liked it to be longer.

War!

Then terror gripped the hearts of all Americans! About one month later Pearl Harbor, Hawaii, was bombed by the Japanese on December 7, 1941. When we left church that Sunday morning, the newsboy was shouting, "Extra, Extra, Pearl Harbor Has Been Bombed." From that day forward, things seemed to be in a whirl. I wondered *what should I do?*

I had already concluded I wanted to have Virgie as my life's companion. One week later on December 14, I proposed marriage to her. She accepted and on April 5, 1942, we were married in that little church on Alston Street in Houston.

Since war was inevitable worldwide, and I was a seventeen years old, I was not old enough to be drafted. I decided I would work wherever I could be of help to the war effort.

Dad went to the Houston shipyard to help in the building of cargo ships, which . were being built in our area. I was not willing to join the shipbuilders, but I became involved in building dormitories at Ellington Field Air Force Base, less than 30 miles from Houston. I became a foreman among the carpenter gang. My pay per hour as a carpenter was more than Dad made at the shipyard. He made $1.75 per hour; I received $1.81 ½ per hour. To say the least, I felt I had arrived. I now made good wages and I was committed to getting married.

Wedding Bells

Wedding day, April 5 arrived quickly. Reverend G. B. Byrne married Virgie and me. I had been acquainted with the Byrne family just after we arrived in Houston. He was a minister who began a new mission church across town from our church, which was west of town.

We rented a small four-room cottage less than a mile from where Mom and Dad lived. We didn't take a honeymoon since I was so occupied in wartime work. The house was new and we were the first occupants. I considered this arrangement would suffice for a honeymoon. I had furnished it with new furniture. As a seventeen year old, I didn't think I was of limited capability to make anything happen for our happiness.

Things have a way of changing with time! In less than three months after marriage, the job at Ellington Field, Air Force Base was finished and I was asked to go to Killeen, Texas, to help construct the dormitory rooms for the Air Force personnel at nearby Fort Hood Army and Air Force Base. Due to the lack of adequate living quarters in Killeen, Virgie was not able to go with me. I went to Killeen with my cousin, Mahlon. We were roommates while on the job at Killeen. He and I had worked together at the Air Base at Ellington.

During the lonely hours after work, I had plenty of time to think. My mind was in a turmoil thinking about all past experiences and I began to focus on the call God had given me when I was just a boy. My job assignment at Killeen was short. When I arrived back in Houston, I reminded Virgie of my call by God and my desire to consider our future objectives.

Camp Meeting Time

The summer of 1942 brought camp meeting time. Virgie and I went to Weatherford that June with Mom and Dad. The campgrounds at Weatherford were large and most attendants camped in tents. One night, unknowingly, I did something I had never done before or since. I got up from my cot and made my way outside. It was only after I had made my way into someone's tent nearby that I heard someone shout at me. Becoming aware that I was sleep-walking, I made a hurried exit back to my own quarters. To say the least, I didn't broadcast my predicament; nor did I ever try to find out whose tent I had entered.

In August 1942, just five months after Virgie and I married, our plans were finalized and I was ready to leave a secular job and begin my studies in religious education to fulfill my calling from God. We sold all of our furniture, packed everything in one suitcase and tied up what we had left in a pillowcase.

A Long Train Ride

To say the least, we did not appear to be very prosperous. Our train left Houston, Texas, for Knoxville, Tennessee, with stops in New Orleans, Birmingham, and Chattanooga. We took a bus on to Sevierville. We were exhausted from traveling but very excited that I was now beginning to answer the call I had from God at age eleven. I was in Bible Training School to study the Bible—"to show myself approved unto God, a workman that needeth not to be ashamed, rightly dividing the Word of Truth" (2 Timothy 2:15). I was about to begin a great new chapter in my life. Even now, when I think of that experience, I get excited! What next?

I had been a dropout from middle school and I didn't know what to expect about the future, but God was allowing me a new location in living and a new life in learning at a school that would be my steppingstone into a fabulous future.

CHAPTER 6

BIBLE TRAINING SCHOOL

"Study to show thyself approved unto God...."
(2 Timothy 2:15).

I was one happy individual! Here I was, a seventeen year old; I had been married six months, and I had plans to enroll in Bible Training School, also known as B. T. S. in Sevierville, Tennessee. I felt like telling the world to open her gates, I was coming through! My call to the ministry five years earlier was now being followed with a new excitement. Virgie and I made plans to enroll in school.

Having dropped out of school after the eighth grade, I did not have a 12th-grade education. To say the least, I had learned through my daily experiences, things I probably would not have learned otherwise. Studying the Bible in a classroom was a great learning experience. My teacher in Personal Evangelism, Avis Swiger, told us the best way to study the Bible was to memorize verses. My first memory verses were Proverbs 3:5-6: "Trust in the Lord with all thine heart, lean not unto thine own understanding, In all thy ways acknowledge Him, and He shall direct thy paths." I was now excited to be in a very special location and receive a very special education. However, it is necessary for a little expansion on this matter.

Bible Training School

The Church of God had established a school to train its ministers and Christian education students in 1918. The school began in Cleveland, Tennessee. In 1932 when Virgie was eight years old, her parents, being in the ministry, moved to Cleveland. She told me how the following conditions affected their family. The uniqueness about this time was that the economic conditions of the depression years adversely affected the housing industry. Reverend W. F. Ainsworth, Virgie's father, and family of four children and Reverend A. V. Beaube with his family of five children, had been longtime friends since their youth. The two preachers had also pastored in Louisiana. They decided to go to Bible School for training in this expanding Church of God school, B. T. S. In order to do this, the two families shared living quarters in Cleveland. In spite of the fact that two families (four adults and nine children) were living together in a house designed for one family, they remained friends. I remember them well.

From Cleveland to Sevierville

During the two decades since its inception, the growth of the student body required a larger facility. So in the late 1930s, the school was moved from Cleveland to Sevierville, Tennessee. The educational facility was on the main street going from downtown Sevierville toward Gatlinburg, the next town. This was a time long before Dolly Parton made Gatlinburg a famous and a desired place to visit. The school complex consisted of one primary building named "Old Main" with two large dormitories on either side. The property was set on a small inclining hill from the main street. The view was quite impressive.

The B. T. S. enrollment in 1942 was approximately 350 students. Since there was only a girls' dormitory and a boys' dormitory, married couples were assigned to the boys' dormitory. There were quite a few married couples.

This location and the living conditions were a lot different than ten years earlier when Virgie's family shared living quarters together. Normally, each dormitory room was designed to accommodate four to six single students. Virgie and I had our private room. I remember we were located across the central hall of the dormitory from a group of six students.

The United States had been at war since December 1941. Having been classified as 4-D (classification for religious deferment) by the Houston draft board, I was soon involved in ministerial studies. I was given my Exhorter Credentials March 2, 1943.

Classes at B. T. S. were either in Christian Education or at the high school level. Since I had not graduated from high school, I enrolled to take a full curriculum in Bible as well as some high school subjects. In the two years I was in Sevierville, I completed sixty semester hours of Bible and finished the ninth grade of high school. I graduated with the class of 1944 with honors.

Being a school where there were a lot of young boys in our dormitory, the ratio of singles to married couples was about four to one. Therefore, it was essential that these young singles be held in check. The boys' dormitory supervisor was Cecil Bridges and his brother, Clifford Bridges, was his assistant. They were obligated to maintain cleanliness and order. Irregularities were always under review. No boy or girl would be allowed to hold hands. To do so, each would be charged with 50 demerits. Any student who received 100 demerits would be sent home. Even as a married couple, we were not permitted to hold hands in public or even walk around the circular drive in front of the campus.

Unexpected 'Twists'

In this part of the story, I faced some complex situations. Upon enrollment, I had paid the tuition for both Virgie and me. After paying the bills, our money was virtually gone. The next twist came when we found out that Virgie was pregnant. What could we possibly do? Just when I thought things couldn't get worse . . . guess what? They did!

Since we had no money, and B. T .S. was closed two weeks for the holidays, we had to stay on campus during that time. The cold weather, no winter wardrobe, and no money kept us inside. The first semester of classes were over just before Christmas. However, just before Christmas day, Cecil Bridges, dormitory supervisor, notified me that I was to have a meeting with President Zeno C. Tharp that morning. We immediately went to the backdoor of President Tharp's home, located just at the end of the boys' dormitory. In spite of the cold weather, there was no invitation to come inside. What happened next was a shock that was just about more than I could stand!

Curt, cutting words from the school president were as follows: "Since you are broke, you don't have money to pay next semester's tuition, your wife is pregnant, and no children may be born in or reside in the boys' dormitory, you must move out of the dormitory now! Furthermore, you are not going to 'make it' anyway, so you might as well pack up and go home."

I was then escorted back to the dormitory to inform Virgie. A very odd condition prevailed during my second year. The ultimatum to vacate the dormitory because no children were allowed to reside there, changed! Cecil and his wife and Clifford and his wife both had babies. Also, since they were dormitory supervisors, they were allowed to remain as residents. Looking back on that now, I wondered about how policies and their enforcement prevails. It was odd.

A New Door

My reaction to this ultimatum was one of shock! But God was about to open a door for us I could not fathom. When I shared the ultimatum with my professor, D. C. Barnes, a new light began to shine. D. C. and Jessie Barnes lived in a small two-room cottage just around the hill from the front of Old Main. Without having to pray over the matter, Professor Barnes took my hand and offered one of those two rooms for our residence. We graciously accepted his offer and continued to live in one room that God and Professor Barnes provided for us for the second semester. We have never forgotten such gracious friends who helped us survive.

At this time, the Tennessee River was being developed in one of its famous TVA projects. The building of a dam across the river had begun and laborers were being hired. I was one of six men from school who went to work on the second shift. I worked from 3 to 11 p.m. daily, arriving home near midnight. Classes began at 7 a.m. This was my schedule for the next five months. I shoveled rock onto the conveyor belt each eight-hour shift, transporting it to the site, a half-mile downstream where the concrete was poured to make a dam to control the river. I slept on a short schedule and made my classes each day from 7 a.m. to 2 p.m. In spite of the president's orders to quit and go home, I adapted to this compressed schedule.

A Family of Three

Time brought the next happy event to reality. All day on April 29, there was evidence of a pending childbirth. When Virgie arrived at the Sevierville Hospital near midnight, her primary doctor was not at home, so an on-duty doctor was called. I was allowed to stay in the delivery room. At 1:30 a.m. on April 30, 1943, with the help of nurses and a physician I did not know, I saw the birth of my son.

School still had less than a month before the semester was over. I was inaugurated in being a father by being tossed into the creek at the back of the B. T. S. buildings by my school friends.

The school year was finally completed. We were now a family of three who had no place to go because we did not have enough money to travel back to Texas. Ten days later, I got a call from the school president. Five months earlier he had given me an ultimatum to leave. Now he called me again into his office. The school board had convened after the school year was finished. Again, I was asked by the president where would I be going for the summer? When I said I have no plans, I was surprised when he said, "Since you have no money and no plans for going home, the board has directed me to give you and Virgie train fare to go to Pennsylvania. There you can work for the summer with one of the board members. He is also the state overseer, Stewart S. Brinsfield."

It was my conclusion that in spite of his previous opinion that, "I wasn't going to make it," I was reclassified. I knew that God's hand was on my life and that my calling was from Him and not man. I knew beyond the shadow of a doubt that the prediction made by the president was not true. Because God was Master of this plan, along with my call to the ministry, I was not promised a path of roses. But I was promised that "All things work together *for good*, (emphasis mine) to them that love God, to those who are the called according to His purpose" (Romans 8:28).

Our First Revival

We traveled to Pennsylvania by train with our two-month-old son, Clayton Duane, along with Reverend Paul and Frances Shoemaker. They were beginning their ministry as pastor, and we would conduct our first revival for them at the Acosta Church. Our second meeting with Brady and Frances Dennis was in Waynesburg, Pennsylvania. A unique side to this event and date is the following. Thirty-six years later, that babe in arms became pastor of Waynesburg during the tenure of overseers, Reverend Earl King and Reverend Terrell Brinson.

We preached at four different churches before camp-meeting time came. Camp meeting at the state office campgrounds was located in Somerset, Pennsylvania. During this era of the 1940 decade, campground facilities were crude. The tabernacle was open-air. The barn that was a part of the campground was converted into sleeping quarters. Reverend Stewart Brinsfield, state overseer, said, "We don't have a hotel to place you in as our state evangelist."

Also, in those days there were no motels. Our place of camp meeting residency was in a barn. The lean-to outside the barn became our sleeping area and the hay trough became the baby's sleeping quarters. For an eighteen year old couple and a three-month-old son to begin evangelism like this made me think that humility can't begin at any lower level.

We received only enough offerings that summer to pay train fare back to Texas. By the time summer was over, we had enough money to get back to B. T. S. for the second term.

When I arrived back at school my second year, I was able to pay part of my tuition by working as a dishwasher in the cafeteria. A compound problem for the school was adapting to the war code. Everything came under government law and food rations, which kept our food at the low minimum of quality. Therefore, the students coined the food name of B. T. S. to mean "Beans, Taters, and Soup."

My extreme delight was my interest in music. I was captivated by music theory, sight-reading, and singing my first year. I had become adept in my music studies. I also became a student of guitar. Teaching guitar the second year helped pay the balance of my tuition. I also was taught to play the accordion. My proficiency in teaching and working in the kitchen never was evaluated.

The second year of school was a very tight schedule. Classes were according to curriculum. Teaching guitar lessons fit in wherever I had open hours. Dishwashing was always a three-times-a-day event. I really didn't have any spare time.

Virgie was interested in completing her senior year of high school. She now had a new baby who kept her busy as a new mom. Being involved in the new schedule, we both had to juggle our time. We lived in a two-room cabin in the same location where we lived our second semester with the Barnes family. Because of this compressed schedule, I was not able to go back to work at the Douglas Dam project.

The first semester of that school year flashed by quickly. It was time to make the Christmas holiday fit into our plans. Virgie's parents had been providing us $5 a month for Duane's milk. Remember, I was not with the "rock gang" eight hours a day. Therefore, that money was not available. Since we had two weeks between first and second semester, Virgie's parents provided her bus fare money to go to Houston.

A Difficult Trip

I was still a hitch-hiker, as we were still at war, and this was the general way for me to travel. What I failed to perceive was that it was December 1943. I did not possess an overcoat. After Virgie and Duane boarded the bus in Knoxville, I headed west. It was less than 150 miles to Nashville. By sundown I was thirty miles east of Nashville at a truck stop. This was a place where truckers did their gas fill-up. No trucker would take a hitch-hiker as a passenger. I was allowed to sit at the restaurant table as though I were a customer, but I was not allowed to sleep inside the premises. It was noon the next day after departing Knoxville that I was able to secure a short ride to get through the city. On the west side of Nashville, I had hoped to find some long-distance travelers who could get me to Memphis.

I was picked-up by a couple of girls. They were very giddy and talkative. As travel got extended, I learned that their interests were not similar to mine. I was being invited to stop, at their discretion, to fulfill their intended proposal. You guessed it. A proposition older than motherhood—prostitution. It was my instant decision to ask that my ride be terminated. I left the car of these two girls and waited until another traveler stopped to offer me a ride. When I got to Memphis I was thirty hours on the road and not halfway to Houston.

My second night on the side of the road was a ditch at the highway's edge. I had not had anything to eat and I still had no cover to sleep. To say the least, my night was full of nightmares as I tried to rest. I did get some long rides on my third day, arriving in Houston tired, exhausted, but glad that I had survived. I never tried to go by thumb again in the winter.

Graduation!
The spring semester of 1944, was back to the same schedule as the first semester. The best thing I recall was that I made new acquaintances. Across the kitchen sink, I met a person who would become my friend. Harold Thompson was renowned because of his bass voice. He was not only a singer, but he also played the trombone, my favorite instrument. Harold sang in a quartet at school. He advanced in the ministry quickly. He was from Arizona. He was two years younger than I and an excellent student in music, studies, friendship, and leadership. Soon the semester would come to a conclusion that all of us were looking for—graduation! I made it.

Now what?

CHAPTER 7

BACK TO TEXAS

"Preach . . . in season, out of season. . . ."
(2 Timothy 4:2).

School, for me, at the present time, was over in the spring of 1944, and I was now a graduate of B. T. S. I was going to begin a brand-new phase of life. As a preacher, I had to search for revival schedules with the state overseer and pastors. Texas was large and churches were many. I wasn't quite sure what I must do to fit into my new position. Because of uncertainty, I took the strength of scripture in 2 Timothy 1:7: "For God hath not given us the spirit of fear; but of power, and of love, and of a sound mind."

Back to Texas

I now had to begin my new activity of collecting all I had accumulated while in Sevierville and head back to Texas. While I had few clothes and few books, I now had a wife and a one-year-old son. The issues in 1944 were the same as 1942 and 1943. I didn't have money. Also, the country was still at war. Since my first year in school, I had personally traveled the way that all males seemed to follow. Everybody—military or civilian—could be seen hitch-hiking. Standing at the side of the road with your thumb held up to your shoulder was the fastest way you might get a ride. I was prepared to send Virgie and Duane to Houston by bus. The ride we traveled together from

Sevierville to Knoxville was by a local bus. I purchased a ticket for Virgie. Duane, being a one-year-old infant, was not charged. When I had them safely on the bus, I waved good-bye as the bus departed from Knoxville. I went to the street and stood with my thumb up. Soon I had a ride. It was a local traveler.

When you are a hitch-hiker, you take whatever ride, without questioning how far that driver is going. The next thing was interesting. As I stood waiting, Virgie's bus came by. I could tell it was the one because I saw the word *Chattanooga* on the front sign of the bus. I saw Virgie holding Duane and I waved as the bus went by. I caught another short ride. Again, I saw her bus and waved as she went by. This happened a total of three times in the short 100 miles between Knoxville and Chattanooga. They got to Houston according to schedule; I arrived late after many long and short trips to make my 900-mile journey. I slept on the side of the road at night when no ride would accommodate me. As a nineteen year old, I believed that if others had to do it to get to their destination, so could I.

I arrived at Mom and Dad's house in Houston and was immediately welcomed by the happy Heil family. Virgie and Duane were there. My brother, Tex, was in the Navy. My next brother, Ed, was preparing to get married. The rest of the family, Mom, Dad, and eight siblings, plus us three, would gather around that long dinner table for Mom's special meals. We did not question how good the food would taste. Our question was, 'Would there be enough in the dish when it came by the others seated at that long table?" Would we have a serving large enough? Sometimes, yes; sometimes, no! When fried chicken was the entree, everybody at the table searched for his or her favorite piece. Not every time was I able to get my chicken leg for dinner.

As a young and inexperienced new graduate and minister, my preaching was unknown to most everyone in Texas. I was dependent upon someone's willingness to welcome me to the pulpit. In those days, the church districts had monthly meetings for fellowship, evangelism, and business. The Houston District was large by geography boundaries. It went as far south as Galveston to as far east as Orange, Texas. I held my first revival in Texas at a little church called *Texla*, near Orange, at the Louisiana border. Hence, the name contracted from Texas and Louisiana—Tex-la.

A New Church

In the summer of 1944, the state overseer asked me if I would be willing to start a church in Beaumont, and I agreed. It should be remembered that the Assembly of God organization was strong in Texas. However, in this 1940 decade, the churches in the Church of God were very small and often weak by comparison.

I was provided a tent and chairs. A lot was obtained. I began advertising and each night I preached only a few people attended. After three weeks, a new episode took effect. Someone came by at night and cut the tent ropes. When I awoke the next morning, I saw my plight. That meant no more services there and my chances of starting a church in Beaumont seemed futile. No future success was evident. I packed my suitcase, put Virgie and Duane on the Greyhound bus, and bought them a ticket back to Houston. I was going to follow them by my regular method—hitch-hiking.

Another 'But-God' Moment

In spite of my financial plight, a strange but extraordinary event took place at the bus stop, halfway to Houston. The bus was loaded with military men who were en route to their assignments. At the café (bus stop), Virgie ordered according to the money she had—one cup of coffee. Duane was less than eighteen months old. He cried for a doughnut. The soldier sitting on a stool next to them said, "Give him a doughnut." He opened the lid where the doughnuts were on the counter and gave it to Duane. His crying stopped, but Virgie was instantly upset. She had only one dime for the coffee. "But God" recognizing this event even before it occurred, provided a nickel. As Virgie stood to pay her bill, she looked down, saw a nickel on the floor, picked it up, paid her bill and excitedly told me later how God provided for her at that moment.

When I arrived home by my hitch-hike method, I heard Virgie's story, and I realized that even when failure in the big things in life occur, the small things will balance the accounts in God's plans. I knew that God could see my circumstances within this Beaumont project. I also would enter the next event I might encounter, remembering that God sees my valley experiences as well as my mountain-top successes. One failure did not have to be my destiny. I fought off the idea that my ministry was finished.

Evangelistic Work

The years 1944 to 1946 were not easy years for me. My adjustment to a new phase in my work was less than normal. I was now intending to be a full-time minister. However, being young and inexperienced, I was not able to obtain a full schedule as an evangelist. I had learned to play the accordion in my second year in Bible School. This made it possible that I could establish my identity, as not only a minister but also as a musician.

Since my father had learned to play the accordion in the 1930 decade, he was always taking his accordion to camp meeting to be a part of the musical team. When I learned to play, I bought my own instrument. At camp meeting I joined the music team, which gave me identity. With my instrument and singing, I soon became recognized.

Since I did not have a schedule that would keep me fully active, I fell back to working in the Houston area in the building industry. Since Dad and all the boys were active in this field, it was not difficult for me to fill my gap in the revival schedule.

One of my interesting times was a revival in San Antonio. The church was small. In fact, it was the first English-speaking church of our denomination in the city. The pastor was building a parsonage at the same time I was invited to preach. The outer shell of the home was complete, but the inside rooms were only identified by the two-by-four studs, which determined the room sizes. There was no sheetrock on the walls. Being a small group and invited to a small church, Virgie, Duane, and I were placed in an area that was separated from the pastor's area by sheets. To say the least, we adapted to that revival schedule with a perplexed mood, yet willing to do what we had to do to become accepted in the Texas evangelism activity.

A Three-Week Revival

Our schedule as evangelists soon expanded. We ultimately were invited to many parts of the state. One of my most exciting times came when a door was opened and the pastor at Iowa Park invited us to come for a revival. We were there for three weeks. It was a great time, working among a strong church group. The pastor, Reverend Jack Gilbert, was a leading pastor in the state. The young people rallied around us. We were a young minister family, twenty-one years old, yet God blessed us with a great revival and converts. I found the results of that revival later. A young boy and girl who received Christ in that revival were married. I saw them often after they married. Years later, I saw that beautiful young couple, called to preach, and serving the Church of God in Tennessee. They are now retired from ministry and reside near Nashville.

To express these references now reminds me that God is the One who directs us, guides us, and helps us along the total pathway of life. While I did not feel that I was called to be an evangelist as my primary ministry, I am thrilled that I can identify three years as an evangelist, and that my ministerial lifespan would be identified with evangelism. I learned what it meant to adapt to the inconsistency of an insecure schedule. I learned how to adapt to the limited income of an evangelist. I became aware of the urgent need to preach the Gospel whenever and wherever the door opens. I learned what it means to be able to work with pastors of different styles, different attitudes, and different demands of a subordinate preacher. I also learned the value of establishing friendship within the ministerial rank, from the lowest in rank to the highest in position. I cherish this status in my ministry. I thought of myself to be a nobody, but after a period of time, effort, sacrifice, devotion, dedication, intent, and commitment, I fulfilled three wonderful years as an evangelist in the state of Texas.

Back to School

During the year I learned that B. T. S. (now Lee College) was moving back to Cleveland, Tennessee. Bob Jones University had been in Cleveland for years and was moving to Greenville, South Carolina. This would be a very good move.

Lee College, named after the Reverend F. J. Lee, second general overseer of the Church of God, would become the flagship school for the church. The school had begun offering college level degrees in education a few years earlier. The third-year level of Christian education was being offered beginning in 1947-1948. I was excited to learn of these changes, believing that this preparation would help me become a better minister and future pastor. These thoughts became driving reasons for me to pull up stakes again and go back to school.

CHAPTER 8

BACK TO SCHOOL

"A workman that needed not to be ashamed...."
(2 Timothy 2:15).

B. T. S. was moving from Sevierville back to Cleveland, Tennessee. Since the school was certified only in the religious education and high school levels, now it was seeking full accreditation at the college level when the fall term of college began. Virgie, Duane, and I became residents of Cleveland, Tennessee, the new home of Lee College. The Cleveland college had the appearance of elegance compared to the school campus at Sevierville. Many of the buildings were of brick structure. However, some of the buildings showed up in the classical wood-framed style of that time.

Providence Hall

The dormitory on 11th Street retained its name, Providence Hall, from the previous residents. It was a two-story, painted, wood-frame unit that housed the married couples that first year. We became residents of Providence Hall. One of the families we met our first month there was Bill, Lorraine, and Christine Alton. Our meeting developed into a lifelong friendship. We only lived in Providence Hall for a short time.

The Battle House

My professor, Reverend D.C. Barnes and his wife and two children had moved into a large two-story house on the corner of 11th and Parker Streets. That house, also known by its former Bob Jones residents as the Battle House, had a vacant second floor. Professor Barnes and his family occupied the lower floor. Because of the friendship Virgie and I had with Professor Barnes and his family during our first years at B. T. S., both families wanted to remain close. So we moved to the second floor in the Battle House until the end of the school year.

My brother, Bud, and I were both entering our third year in Lee College. Because the two of us were in school together, we became very close. It so happened that both of us were in charge of the campus maintenance. We were also a team who built the stage props for the plays that were produced.

Even though the college rules mandated strict compliance to campus regulations, on the weekends, we were privileged to attend the churches in Cleveland. Living one block from the North Cleveland Church of God was a special treat for us. The Reverend James L. Slay, and his wife, Ruby, had been pastor there since 1943. I note this timeframe because it would become a special identification in later years as our paths crossed.

As I was enrolling in classes for my studies at Lee, I became aware that the curriculum for my third year of Christian education was the same curriculum as the first year of college studies. I asked questions of those who were assigned to process me about the relative similarity. I was immediately directed to see the dean, Dr. E. M. Tapley. I informed Dr. Tapley that I would like to receive college credit for my studies, but that I was not a high school graduate. I had only finished the ninth grade while I was a student at B. T .S. in 1942-1944. I also told him I did not have my GED certificate. After reviewing my grade point average, Dr. Tapley said, "If you will take the subjects for the college level and pass the classes, I will give you college credit."

I was now in a high mood of excitement. Not only was I about to begin my ministerial study, but I would also receive college credit. Time was in my corner. I settled into my studies with utmost diligence. At the end of the school term, my thirty credit hours revealed a grade of "A" in all classes.

Becoming a Full-Time Minister

When I concluded my first college year in 1948, Virgie, Duane, and I returned to Texas. I was twenty-three years old. I was now looking forward to a time in my life when I would be able to reach my goal—that of becoming a full-time minister—my calling.

When Virgie, Duane, and I returned to Houston, I wanted to enroll at the university there, but it was necessary that I become employed in order to pay for continued schooling.

The Heil family in Houston had survived the war with no fatalities. All of my brothers were now based in Houston, working as contractors. Dad had become partners with Bud; Jebo partnered with Darvel, Punk, Fitty, David, and Dan. When I came back from Tennessee, I joined with Tex. Work was plentiful because Houston was a booming city. Our father had taught his nine sons how to build. Now all of us, including Dad, were successful contractors.

My First Real Estate Venture

From 1949 to 1951 I was blessed by having lots of work. During that time, I was made aware of a proposed road expansion coming through East Houston, so I bought two small buildings and had them moved to a lot I had purchased in northeast Houston in a subdivision called Kashmere Gardens. The total price of the two units, plus moving, was $2,000. I added a room and made the first unit a five-room home. The second unit, I elevated with special cribbing to an eight-foot height and made it a garage apartment with an outside landing and steps to the ground. This was my first venture in real estate This project made me a homeowner. My total mortgage price for the lot with improvements was $3,500. I was able to work, pay my mortgage, and pay my tuition without any problems. This plan allowed me to continue my work schedule and my school schedule.

My schedule worked out so I could attend evening classes at the University of Houston. I would be at my construction work at seven in the morning and work until 2 p.m. I would then go home for supper, leave home, and drive to class at 4 p.m. I did not consider this routine difficult because I knew it was fulfilling my purpose.

A Miracle of Healing

At this point, I will deviate to share a fabulous experience. Sometime during my previous time in Cleveland, I discovered a hernia in my left groin. Because of my tight schedule, I would not take time to have it surgically repaired. The only other alternative was to wear a hernia belt. I did this now for almost two years.

In Houston, as well as across the nation, the church world was ablaze with big-name evangelists. One of these evangelists was Oral Roberts. He was conducting a tent meeting in North Houston. His huge tent was always packed with people. Virgie and I could only attend the meeting on Saturday and Sunday nights because of my tight schedule.

One Sunday evening we arrived at the meeting early. In deep dedication, I exercised my faith. I asked God to heal my hernia. Before I ever arrived for service, I had removed my hernia belt. After Evangelist Roberts finished his sermon, he called for those who needed healing to come to the front of the tent. Before I could get to the front where he was anointing each person, I felt a divine touch. I was healed. In my ecstasy, I jumped for joy and shouted, "I'm healed! I'm healed!"

The next day, I was working on a house, standing on a scaffold set to the side of the wall. Al Statum, my brother-in-law, was my helper. We were putting asbestos siding over the wood siding. I said to Al, "I got healed last night of my hernia. Look, I can jump from the scaffold, and I don't have the evidence of the bulging hernia that I have had so long." I jumped to show him the reality of my declaration. All was wonderful.

However, on Wednesday afternoon at 3:30 as we were eating supper, I said to Virgie, "I lost my healing today."

In shock, Virgie pushed her chair back and said, "I'm not eating!" The next few minutes were a whirl. Virgie said, "Last Sunday in my prayer, I said, 'O God, if you will heal Wayne, I will be willing to fast three days without food or water.'" She left the table and went to our bedroom to pray.

For the rest of that week I did not put on the hernia belt, and I suffered the bulging of that hernia as I continued to do my 15-hour work and college schedule. On Sunday, we went back to the tent meeting. While in that healing line the second time, I felt the divine flush feeling over my body. Again, I was healed! That was sixty-one years ago. I have never put that hernia belt back on and doctors who have examined me many times since have declared that I do not have any evidence of having had a groin hernia. Thank God!

I was a successful building contractor. I was making money and was able to pay my way in all of my building activities as well as my college tuition. Yet, after finishing my second year of college in Houston, I had a strong feeling that I should be in full-time ministry.

My First Pastorate

I decided to talk to the state overseer about my calling and my feelings when he came to Houston for the annual District Convention. I had met Brother Aultman earlier when he was state overseer of New Mexico in 1944 to 1946. He served four years as overseer of Kentucky and was now in his final two years as overseer of Texas.

Brother Aultman was a very cordial and friendly leader. He gave special attention to my conversation. I discussed with him my feelings about wanting to be in ministry full time and pastoring a church. When I finished my appeal, he said, "I will help you." This appeal was in the spring of 1951. I informed Brother Aultman that at camp-meeting time, I would come prepared to go to my assignment as a pastor.

I sold my contracting business to my brother Tex. I packed personal belongings in my new Nash automobile and arrived in Weatherford at camp meeting. Brother Aultman informed me that I would be the pastor of the church at Strawn, Texas, a little town of 500 people about fifty miles west of Weatherford. I had remembered the name, *Strawn*, because two very talented guitar students named *Gibson* had come to B. T. S. in Sevierville when I was a student there. This memory of the Gibson brothers gave me the feeling that the church had recognition. I was in a happy mood because I was soon to be a pastor.

Later I learned that the membership in the Strawn church was very small and its attendance was the same. Virgie, Duane, and I were leaving Houston. We had been off-and-on residents there for over twelve years. We had lived two of those years in Sevierville, Tennessee, as students at B. T .S. and one year at Lee College in Cleveland, Tennessee. Now I was soon to find out how life was to be in the sagebrush area of Texas, in the little town named *Strawn*.

This was a new turn in my life's journey—to be pastor of a church and be able to lead them in their spiritual journey. I also wanted to understand the complex issues of a valley experience and yet to be able to rejoice when they rejoiced. When my stomach butterflies brought me to question my capabilities, I prayed for wisdom and strength. **BUT GOD** was to enter all of the situation very shortly and turn all of the issues around and start me on a brand-new course of my life. My stability crutch was found in Paul's admonition in Ephesians 6:10: "Be strong in the Lord, and in the power of his might."

CHAPTER 9

WOW!

"And we know that all things work together for good. . . ." (Romans 8:28)

Camp meetings in Texas have always been noted for being great, exciting, and very spiritually rewarding. Camp-meeting time in Weatherford brought members from ninety-four Texas congregations to this tabernacle where worshipers had come for many years. Camp meeting enthusiasm and friendship renewals were always at a high peak. I attended my first camp meeting in Weatherford, Texas, in 1940 and continued to attend the Weatherford campground until it was sold in 1950. I thought this place was next to heaven. It became apparent that the old campground and tabernacle needed improvements. A decision was made to relocate the state offices and campground to Fort Worth.

After the state office purchased a large property in Fort Worth, it became a choice parcel of land for the expanding General Motors plant. Brother Aultman, the Texas overseer, along with the consent of the state council made the decision to sell. A huge profit from that Fort Worth sale made it possible to go back to a large acreage three miles east of Weatherford and build the new campground debt free. When the total project was analyzed, it was concluded that Brother Aultman needed help to complete this new project before he would leave Texas. Due to church limitation rules in the general polity provision, he only had one year left of his two-year term.

A New Spiritual Road

In the middle of the camp meeting week in June 1951, the state overseer came to me after the afternoon service had concluded. Brother Aultman was very speedy in his remarks to me. "Wayne, your assignment to be pastor of the church at Strawn has changed; you are no longer assigned as pastor there. As of this moment, by my authority and the authority of the state council, you are the new youth director of the state of Texas. I need a builder! We have a new project to complete, a new campground."

I was overwhelmed! My pastoral dream had exploded. My mental response was *Why?* I didn't know what to say. I didn't know how to respond. **But God** in His divine purpose was about to open new doors and direct me down new roads I had never dreamed could occur in my life and ministry. My goal six months earlier was to become a pastor, **But God** who foreknows everything was now revealing His purpose to me at this time and was about to lead me on a new spiritual road.

I began reviewing my Texas maps to locate the ninety-four Church of God congregations in the state. I learned it was 1,000 miles from east to west and 1,000 miles from north to south in traveling across Texas. I was reminded of the little poem I had heard some years before by an unknown author. His poetry was very archaic. It went like this: "The sun has riz, and the sun has set, and here we is, in Texas yet."

My travels extended to the 94 churches in Texas in one year. One unusual experience happened in Fort Worth in

1952. I had a bad headache after Sunday morning service. I decided to stop for help at a local drug store to find relief. I went to the counter and asked for a glass of water and I bought an Alka-seltzer. I tore open the paper and removed the pill. I placed it on my tongue and took a fast swallow of water. Virgie, in shock said, "What did you do?"

When I told her my story, I had an instant reaction. I began to belch and the gassy Alka-seltzer began spewing from my stomach. For the next three hours I thought I had a "gas well" exploding in me. Forever after, I have been allergic to any kind of aspirin-content medicine.

A New Campground in Texas

My work schedule had to be such so that I would spend five days each week on the campground job site. Leaving late Friday afternoons, I would travel to a nearby church for Friday night service. Saturday and Sunday would find me at a further distance on my preaching ministry. I had to be back in Weatherford for Monday morning's new work schedule.

Not only was I to be a state youth director, I was also to be the superintendent to oversee the construction of the new tabernacle, the focal point of this whole new venture. As stated on a previous page of this chapter, the church state board decided to move the state headquarters offices to Fort Worth. That conclusion was reversed as defined earlier. The reasons for the decision were because of money and time. The board realized that to build in Fort Worth would have been conditioned by multiple building code laws. Also, other regulations that might be necessary to have approval could impede the construction before

Brother Aultman's tenure limitation would prevail. Consequently, the state council, along with the overseer, decided to buy a large portion of land three miles east of Weatherford where no code restraints would apply.

Many acres of property within the compound were provided to accommodate residents who wished to own their homes on the campground. This would be similar to the Wimauma Campground in Florida. Also, the area would contain the state offices, parsonages for the overseer and state youth director, and a large new closed-in air-conditioned tabernacle. In the planning would be all the necessary auxiliary buildings. One great plus that determined this move was that there would not be any city inspectors determining code regulations.

The total plan for the campground had been established and would take shape as speedily as each phase demanded. Roads were cut by bulldozers, and blacktop was applied. The water lines were established as soon as a deep-water well was drilled. Electric lines were run throughout the grounds. Ministers began to make plans for their personal residences. I started my own building immediately on the very first lot designated for camp-ground cottages. It was a small four-room house with a bath.

The tabernacle was designed to be the focal point of the grounds. Other buildings would be built to serve in their capacity. A dining hall was nearby. The state office for administrative work was adjacent to the plot set aside for the overseer's residence. Special parking areas were set up for all vehicles that must be accommodated for the large auditorium.

The beautiful part of this plan was that the overseer wanted all the activity necessary to bring the property to active function by the date he was to leave Texas, which was one year later. Having been in my capacity as a person who had built all types of structures, I was challenged with the requirement to accomplish this task.

I had been a very proficient contractor in the Houston area for a number of years. I had been blessed in my financial status in Houston. My income had averaged $600 per month. I was so excited about my new assignment of becoming state youth director, I did not question what the position would pay. I was soon to learn, however, that my pay for performing the dual job of serving as state youth director and completing the campgrounds during the next twelve months would be the sum of $200 per month. Wow! **But God** again knew my life. He would be showing me that I did not need to determine my financial security through my activity, but I would be provided for if I would keep my trust in Him.

The year passed swiftly. The campgrounds were completed on schedule, and as youth director, I organized the second youth camp in Texas. I felt honored that I was able to obtain Dr. Hollis Gause as our guest speaker.

With the completion of his assignment as overseer, Brother Aultman was reassigned to the Alabama City Church in Alabama. He had been pastor of that church eight years before he became a state overseer. In order to be prepared for the General Assembly in Indianapolis, Brother Aultman left Weatherford a week early, leaving me with necessary instructions for completing specific duties. After finishing local tasks, Virgie, Duane, and I drove toward the General Assembly site. As I drove through the city of St. Louis, I found my mood was affected by the dirty appearance of that city. After we left the city and crossed over into the state of Illinois, I said to Virgie, "If the good Lord helps me, I will never set foot in that city again."

Indianapolis, in 1952, did not have a convention center. The General Assembly convened in a very large complex called the *Fairgrounds*, two miles north of the downtown area. Our hotel accommodations, not being close to the Fairgrounds, mandated travel by car to get back and forth each day where business and worship services were held.

Tremont Avenue Church of God

The General Assembly concluded on Sunday at noon. The Texas ministers convened in the assigned location to welcome the newly appointed overseer, the Reverend J. D. Bright. I was reappointed as state youth director for the next two years. I spent an hour after the close-out of our Texas group looking for Brother Aultman. I was wanting to be sure that I would be able to make Brother Bright's arrival to Texas an easy process. After searching that huge compound for an hour; finally, our paths crossed.

Brother Aultman shocked me again! I recall how dramatic and emphatic his comments were: "Wayne, I have changed your assignment. You are no longer youth director of Texas; I want you to go to South Carolina. Go down this hall and at a certain door you will knock. Go in and say to the person inside, I am your man. You will be talking to the Reverend A. M. Phillips, pastor of the Tremont Avenue Church."

I told Brother Aultman, "I have not prayed about changing my assignment. I have just been reappointed youth director. Further, I have not talked to Virgie about a change."

"There is no time to talk to your wife, no time to pray, just do as I say." There were men standing at his door wanting to be interviewed and to get his agreement and assignment to be assistant pastor at the Tremont Avenue Church.

I was shocked! WOW! Again, God was changing the direction of my life and the road to my future. But God is now showing me through his servant ministers how He can direct us if we are willing to accept it.

Standing in line were people I did not know. However, the first person waiting for an interview was Walter R. Pettitt. When I knocked on the door, a man in a beautiful white suit shook my hand. I told Brother Phillips, a person I had never met before that day, "I am your man." Within minutes he informed me of his intentions and would contact his council that afternoon to confirm his decision to employ me as his associate.

A Prayer Answered–Eight Years Later

In 1943-44, during a fall convocation at B. T .S., the Reverend Frank Spivey was the speaker at that event. During the convocation each night I was excited about Brother Spivey's preaching. His cordiality also intrigued me. I prayed to the Lord and said, "If I can just become capable of being the same kind of person and leader as Brother Spivey and become the assistant pastor at Tremont Avenue, I will be happy."

That afternoon, eight years after that prayer, I was informed that my assignment was confirmed. I was the assistant pastor of Tremont Avenue Church of God in Greenville, South Carolina. At that time, Tremont Avenue was considered to be the largest church in the Church of God—nationwide. WOW! But God again directed and I accepted His will in my life and my appointment. Time passed swiftly. I had to go back to Texas and pack and be in my new assignment in two weeks.

CHAPTER 10

TREMONT AVENUE— GREENVILLE, SOUTH CAROLINA

"New things are come to pass...."
(Isaiah 42:9).

Greenville, South Carolina, is a beautiful city. The northern part of the state is largely influenced by the cotton-mill industry that abounded in Greenville during the 1950s. It had been known for decades as a cotton-mill town. The people of that city were very competent in producing cloth from the weaving of cotton.

I am not knowledgeable of the leadership of the original pastor of this renowned church, which was organized in 1919. In the 1930s and 1940s the church attendance exploded under the leadership of two great men, the Reverends Zeno C. Tharp and Earl P. Paulk. A new church was built in Greenville during the 1940 decade that had a seating capacity of 1,000. The Greenville congregation called Reverend A. M. Phillips who was pastor of a church in Atlanta to become pastor of this great church. When I came to Tremont in 1952, the membership was 950. I was given instructions by Brother Phillips to serve the congregation with my visits to homes and hospitals without regard to prior reviewing of schedules with him. Brother Phillips explained the simplicity of my duties. He said, "Wayne, you are to consider half of the membership to be your area of service and I will serve the other half."

Learning from the Best

I was able to learn a special kind of knowledge in my new assignment, which was to serve in any area of need. It would be considered to be proper activity. I was privileged to sit in on the counsel sessions of the church. I was the secretary who kept the minutes of the counsel's business meetings. Listening to the pros and cons of business and how the decisions were drawn from these sessions was an experience I didn't learn from a book. I derived this knowledge by being a part of the activity.

In my time at Tremont in this area of service, I felt as though I had been in another university class. I learned ethics and business principles from A to Z. More than that, I became aware of the intricate relationship that prevails between parties in the reaction to or rejection of authority. I learned from observation the conditions that council members must consider and what conclusions are made between them. I began to interpret the issues as I saw them. I concluded that policies were affected by policymakers. Often, I found that the polity was modified to accommodate the majority group. This may not have been the best end-result, but it became the law. More about this in later chapters.

Bobby Gene Heil

During my first year at Tremont, Virgie and I had another child. Virgie had miscarried at five months in Texas the year before. This baby was a boy, but due to Virgie's heart trouble, she could not carry him to term. She had the premature birth at six months. Our infant son was born alive but lived only four hours. Bobby Gene was buried in a cemetery in North Greenville near Bob Jones University. This sorrow continued to prevail in our lives because our family happiness continued to be drastically affected by life and death in very swift proximity. We asked ourselves how much more can we endure?

Let me remind you of my emphasis in the introduction to these chapters. Sometimes the despair of valley experiences occur, and I have wondered why they must be. Then mountaintop ecstasy conditions occur. I know that God does understand and that He cares about all of my experiences, circumstances, and situations.

I had recalled from Brother Spivey's ministry eight years earlier when he came to B. T. S. about the spiritual emphasis in worship at Tremont. I was now in this wonderful and happy ministry and worship every week. I especially recall the time when Evangelist J. K. Thibideau preached a revival at Tremont. Duane received his Holy Ghost Baptism during that revival.

We lived across the street from the Tremont church in the back rooms of the building where the Ladies Willing Worker Band served monthly meals. The ladies were wonderful cooks and the food was delicious. I remember especially the good fried chicken and sweet potato casserole.

I didn't have any stressful feelings about my income. I was paid $75 per week as my salary. In addition to my duties as assistant pastor, I was to use my knowledge of building in the new parsonage project. However, that part of the plan did not materialize during my tenure.

What happened next during my tenure at Tremont was a new episode in my life. Ten months after my arrival,

Brother Phillips was called by the General Church officials to leave Tremont to become state overseer of Kentucky. I was now interim pastor for six weeks. The new pastor was appointed by due process. The selection was a wonderful decision. Reverend James L. and Ruby Slay were appointed the new pastors at Tremont. They were coming from South Africa. The Slay family had been under General Church assignment as ambassadors to the newly amalgamated church in South Africa. They were in South Africa thirteen months before this new appointment.

I was now under new tutorship. Brother Slay was a different type leader than Brother Phillips. You might say that they were opposites. Whereas Brother Phillips was openly casual, Brother Slay was creatively brilliant in his ministry ethics, with simple understanding to comprehend and act punctually in his function. My family and I were pleased to have companionship with the new pastor. The Slay family were four in number: James L., Ruby Lee, James L. Jr. (Rusty) and Jerry. Virgie and I were more than ten years younger than the Slays. However, Duane and Rusty were only one year different in age. Jerry was three years younger. Duane was nine, Rusty was eight, and Jerry was five. The kids went to school nearby, and we were happy for our children's pleasant relationship with each other.

Mission Board Appointment

Three months after the Slay family came to Tremont, I had a special event that drastically affected me. One evening I received a phone call from Reverend Earl P. Paulk, chairman of the World Mission Board. They were in their fall business session (September 28-30, 1953). He was swift in his conversation. He came right to the point.

The Mission Board has asked that you go to Haiti to serve as the overseer and also to build a new Bible School. Will you accept? I was speechless.

The night before, I had read an article from the *Reader's Digest* magazine. The magazine story told of the first dry-cleaning facility that had opened just weeks earlier in Port-au-Prince, Haiti. I remembered that story when Brother Paulk called.

I responded to Brother Paulk in this manner: "Brother Paulk, I have not been called by God to be a missionary. Are you asking me to go anyway? If I go, I will need to have time to consider this request. How much time do I have to answer you?"

His reply was, "Tomorrow!"

The next morning I went to the office. I found Brother Slay studying for his next sermon. I unloaded the whole story of what happened the night before. I asked him if he thought I should consider this call?

Our conversation was dead serious. To go to Haiti I knew I would have to leave Tremont, the place where I said in my prayers eight years earlier I wished to be. I then asked Brother Slay, "How do I know if this is God's will?"

His answer was, "God works through servants. If they determine a reason and devise a proposal of this nature, I would consider it to be God's will." I still was not sure of what I needed to do. Brother Slay told me, "Go talk to the state overseer, James A. Cross."

I left the Tremont office and drove to the state office four miles away and met with Brother Cross. I had known Brother Cross since I was a boy. In fact, he was the pastor of the Mobridge church in the mid-1930s. However, eighteen years later, I was now a grown man and had my history of various assignments in the Church of God. I was humbled to hear the decision of my overseer: "If the Church Mission Board has decided they need you and you accept the request, consider it God's will. I will release you from your appointment in due process."

At two o'clock that afternoon, the phone rang. It was Brother Paulk. He asked me what was my decision? I answered, I have some conditions. His response was okay. "The Board meets at seven o'clock tonight. You have five hours to get here from Greenville."

At seven o'clock I was sitting outside the board conference room in Cleveland, Tennessee. At eight thirty, the board members heard my questions. Then the issues began to get fuzzy. One of the members asked if I would go to the Middle East (Israel and the surrounding countries) and be the superintendent of that area. I would be stationed in Jerusalem. My response was quick. "I thought you were wanting me to go to Haiti?"

The issues quickly reverted to Haiti. I asked, "If I accept, how soon do I have to be in Haiti? Second, is there a school for my nine-year-old son who must receive his schooling in the English language?"

The first answer was: "As soon as you can get passports, process for visas, get tickets and arrange all other necessary situations to arrive at your earliest. About the school, we understand that a new school is opening in January for all foreign language students.

I responded that I felt I must have three months to make this transition. I was pleased to learn of the school situation. If this would be acceptable, I feel I would be in God's will.

My questions continued. "Why are you sending me?" Here the issues came to light. The Mission Board had asked Brother Aultman to go to Haiti and build a Mission Compound because they knew he had built the campground complex in Texas two years earlier. Brother Aultman quickly answered, "I got the credit but the person who did the job is the one you need to send."

The board continued with their story. "Brother Aultman has recommended you and we accept you. James Beaty, our missionary to Haiti has purchased a large parcel of land two and one-half miles from downtown Port-au-Prince. There has been a plan from Haiti for many months to educate the Haitian students to become ministers for the Lord to reach the people of Haiti with the Gospel. Brother Beaty is an educator; he is not a builder."

The questions posed by me and the responses given by the board seemed satisfactory. Forty-eight hours from the time I had read an article about a dry-cleaning business in Haiti, my whole life was headed in a different direction. I was to be a missionary, an overseer of over 100 churches, more than 150 ministers, with a membership of 7,500, and a designated builder of a fabulous mission compound. Because of church polity and related policy, I did not yet have the required years designated to be an ordained minister. My eligibility for ordination required that I be thirty years of age. I was only twenty- eight years old.

Changing Locations

I went home to Tremont and began the process of obtaining passports and visas. The time factor of getting the government to issue these legal documents took more than two months. At this time, I began locating material to build a large freight container. I calculated the items we would have to send according to Brother Beaty. When I finished building the freight box, it was eight feet long, three feet wide and six feet tall. It took a truck to transport it to the freight station. Shipping by freight would take six weeks. Two weeks before Christmas we were finally cleared to fly with valid visas and passports. Brother Beaty suggested that we spend the holidays with family. Because we called Texas home since marriage, we went back to Texas for our final visit there. Beaty recommended that we wait until New Year's to arrive. That was exactly three months and one day from the date of the appointment to go to Haiti. I concluded: "It is God's will."

Does God do drastic things? Do those things happen to ordinary people? Are all the little things that happen to an individual a part of God's overall program? If the answers seem uncertain or maybe incomplete, just wait. I wondered, but God directed and I submitted. In looking back, I say to you, I have been there, done that! This is my life. I will now become a missionary. Because not only will I build a compound, but I will also learn the French and Creole language to permit me to preach the Gospel to some of the finest, humblest, conscientious people in the Western Hemisphere! My story continues!

CHAPTER 11

MISSIONS

"Go into all the world, and preach the gospel"
(Mark 16:15).

What makes a man a missionary? First comes a call. When a person seeks God for His direction, it often comes through prayer or some spiritual revelation. In my case, the call came through a contact and decision of a special board whose total objectives were to sow the seed of the Gospel through men appointed by them to accomplish that task. When I accepted that appointment, my world expanded with a new vision and purpose. I was, from that day forward, a missionary.

I learned that the word *mission* has many definitions. To organize or establish a mission among a people or a territory is one definition from the dictionary. However, the plural of the word and its meaning brings this word to a much broader expansion. When Jesus gave this declaration, it was meant to be the method of reaching all the world with the Gospel.

In my research, I found that Church of God World Missions outreach began in 1911 in the Bahama Islands. The expansion of missions grew as ministers went from island to island to preach the Gospel. The *Webster Dictionary* defines the Caribbean Sea as a 750,000 square miles extension of the Atlantic Ocean, bounded by the coasts of Central and South America and the major islands of the West Indies.

While continuing my study about missions, I found this theme was the primary objective of the church. Stateside growth reached many states since our missions outreach four decades earlier. World Missions was our adopted term to express any area outside of the United States. While mission growth expanded dramatically to many countries of the world, the West Indies was the area that grew most swiftly.

Church of God ministers were encouraged to visit a mission territory to learn of the people, their needs, and how to support and help them survive. To get to these islands, one would arrange a schedule that would allow a visit to five different islands. Leaving Miami, the first stop was Puerto Rico, followed by stops in Dominican Republic, Haiti, Jamaica, Cuba, and then back to Miami. The cost for this circular trip was $225. This adventure by plane with stops to these islands was promoted by the World Missions Department as the best method to indoctrinate and build the expansion of missions.

The World Mission's Board had been advised by James Beaty that some kind of expansion, by way of education, must be given for the mission program in Haiti to grow. James Beaty was an educator who proposed that a parcel of land be obtained and a mission compound be built. In correspondence to Beaty, on February 9, 1953, the board agreed to buy a large parcel of land in a location called *Bourdon*.

From this action, decisions were followed to obtain someone who could build that compound. Beaty's correspondence to me pinpointed the board's action. It was an order of the day for 1:30 p.m. Tuesday, September 29,

1953, to decide on the Haiti proposition. The conditions unfolded in the following manner:

A member recommended Wayne Heil for the overseership of Haiti because of his knowledge of building, and so forth.

1. That A. M Phillips call Wayne Heil and ask him if he would be interested in being considered as the superintendent of Haiti.
2. Wayne Heil came before the board at their request to be interviewed for Haiti and the Middle East.
3. When the Middle East position was brought up, no action was followed, since the Haiti proposition was the only one discussed by phone the day earlier.
4. The final act was concluded in the following manner: That we appoint Wayne Heil and wife as the overseer of Haiti and that his probationary term be considered three years at the salary of $180 per month, plus child allowance according to the policy.

On October 5, 1953, James Beaty was informed by Executive Missions Secretary, Paul H. Walker, of my appointment to Haiti. The emphasis of the decision by the board gave Haiti and the missionaries a state of excitement. The correspondence from Beaty was now concrete in defining their future.

When we were informed that our passports and visas had been issued, we left the assignment we had at the Tremont Avenue Church to enter our new assignment. We arrived in Port au Prince, Haiti, on December 31, 1953. Meeting us at the airport and assisting us in the chore of clearing customs were James and Virginia Beaty and Odine Morse. They were, by board appointment, missionaries to Haiti. Virgie and I felt a strange yet wonderful feeling. We had been appointed as overseer of the Church of God in Haiti. Now we became foreign residents on an island of four million people.

Port-au-Prince

Brother Beaty, by approval of the Mission's Board, had purchased fifteen acres of land earlier that year. It was approximately three miles from the ocean in the city of Port-au-Prince, Haiti. The elevation of the property was 1,500 feet above sea level. On this site was to be built three missionary homes, an office, and a Bible School complex to include classrooms, chapel, library, dormitories, dining room, kitchen, and so forth. What had been a dream in the mind of James Beaty was about to blossom into reality.

Arriving on the last day of the year became an historic reference to me. I had informed the Missions Board that I felt it would be the "will of God" if I should have three months to finalize my work at Tremont, prepare for my transition, obtain passports and visas, and get to my new assignment within that time element. If you look back at the calendar of events, you will find it was exactly three months from my being appointed until setting foot on the soil of my new home.

The mood of excitement prevailed from day one. The Beaty home was about to have an explosion of occupants. Bill and Lorraine Alton and daughter Christine, and Faye Singleton, missionaries from the Dominican Republic, were celebrating the Christmas and New Year holiday with the Beatys and Odine Morse. Dominican Republic is that portion of the island on the opposite end of the Hispaniola Island of which Haiti is a part. We arrived the day before the New Year of 1954. Two days later, four more visitors from the mainland were among those who sought a place to make their bed at bedtime at the Beaty compound in Petionville.

Renewed Friendships

We were seeking to know how to fit into this jig-saw puzzle. It was not difficult. Having been school buddies with the Altons gave us close friendship again. Faye Singleton was a member of the Houston church when we lived there. I was a classmate in school with Virginia (Green) Beaty ten years earlier. Now we were about to find the fellowship and friendship of people we had known for a long time.

A rental residence was secured for us by James Beaty three blocks from their home in Petionville. This community was about five miles from the seacoast and bordered Port-au-Prince. The elevation at Petionville was 2,500 feet above sea level. Even though we were to live in the tropics and it would always be summertime, the blessing of upper elevation and cool winds always made it more comfortable.

Language School

Our first obligation was to begin language study. Haiti was an occupied country by France for 200 years prior to their independence, and French was the official language of the land. But because Haiti had become an occupied country by slaves from Africa, the language of the people was Creole. My first chore was to begin my study of French and Creole. My teacher was a Haitian of good education who was also a member of the government. This teacher not only taught me French and Creole, but he also guided me on how obtain government documents to import necessary materials without having to pay the exorbitant duty fees.

My first year in Haiti was exciting. James and Virginia Beaty were so supportive. They helped us when it became necessary to participate in church services and business within the ministry. James was a very great linguist. He had first served in the Dominican Republic as a missionary before being assigned to Haiti. He was fluent in Spanish and French. Every time I was to be in a church activity, James was my translator when I preached. He was also my guide when I needed his wisdom relating to my obligations and duties as a leader. We traveled together in virtually every schedule I made. His insight in the needs of the Mission Compound Project became my guidelines that I was to follow toward completion of the total project.

The authorization to do the project was approved by the church in America, but now we had to follow through with the governmental authority of Haiti. Getting permits was the starting point. Beaty and I were continually at the Palace. This building not only served as the residence of the king (ultimately dictator) of the country, but the building also contained the legislative branch of government authority. To obtain licenses and permits to fulfill this dream of James Beaty's required a high level of achievement. I became acquainted with people of high authority. I began to function in my capacity as overseer of a dynamic church. I also quickly adapted in my capacity as builder after I had been there only six months. Of course I had to speak Creole daily to the populace and French to the government leaders.

What was of great value to me was the ability to identify the goals to be achieved for the mission work of Haiti. The first act of physical work on the fifteen acres was to obtain a road access up to the property from the area road next to a stream on the back side of our property. We obtained a D-8 bull dozier and I soon learned how to operate that large machine. I had to learn its function and access the land from lower stream level to a plateau where our compound was soon to be.

Hit by Lightning

One early experience on this compound occurred after we had obtained our electricity from across the valley. I had built a small tool shed—10 square feet—and was just finishing it for use. On that day, one of the frequent rain showers with a sizable amount of lightning and thunder occurred. I was standing three feet from the electric pole and ten feet from the tool shed when I was "hit" by a lightning strike. If I had not been wearing thick rubber-soled shoes, I suppose I might have been killed. After the storm was over, the inspector found that the transmitter serving our plateau had been knocked out by the storm. The authorities told me that it was a 7,200 volt transmitter. You might draw a conclusion about this incident. Either the Enemy, who would desire my demise, or the Lord, who took care of me so that I could continue my task, was in control of that situation.

I learned the locations of the building suppliers and very soon was knowledgeable of the people who soon were eager to sell me supplies to build the Mission Compound. These people knew very well where I would be able to obtain the right material from any foreign country and at the right price. This would allow me to import whatever I needed in the quickest time possible. Since Haiti was a land with very little timber to manufacture a finished lumber product, virtually all the wood for building purposes had to be imported.

The Haitian laborers had become adept at making concrete blocks. A block mold allowed the laborers to mix the proper proportion of sand, cement, and water to make the blocks necessary to complete a building. Virtually all buildings in the island countries are made of concrete material.

Because the temperature is always hot, it is a wonderful situation when the cool breezes blow. This condition enters into the concept of the building under construction. The widows were metal frames and the glass was Venetian blind type. Since there is no need for heat to any building, all of the construction had these type of windows. This allowed for instant cool air as needed.

A strange event took place at our residence after we moved into our house. One morning when we awoke, we discovered all the sheer curtains that graced our living room had been cut off about six inches from the top. The thief had used his knife to cut off the very beautiful sheers, and without making a noise, he was gone and never apprehended.

Another Loss

Another event of meaningful emphasis relates to how life unravels. On February 14, 1956, infant Larry Dale was born and lived three hours. This was the third loss of an infant for Virgie and me. To commemorate him, we placed his casket in the curve of the road leading up into the compound and placed a flat gravestone to mark the burial place. Many people have commented to us over the years of that special place on the compound.

My first year in Haiti was multifaceted. Keeping the church-work in order with 150-plus ministers who were leaders in 105 churches and more than fifty mission stations was the first order of activity. With legal and regulatory policy about the new buildings, waterlines and roadwork kept me busy. There was no time for loafing.

Seeing the beautiful land and the wonderful people who treated us like kings and queens made our lives exciting. The northern area of Haiti had a very large territory that was developed by one of Haiti's first kings, Dessalines, when they achieved independence in the late 1700s. In Cape Haitian province, a large fortress called the *Citadel* was constructed as a defense against the country's recapture by any foreign nation. When the Beatys took us to see that historic fortress, we felt like we were 150 years back in time. To see the dozens of cannons in the walls of that fortress and piles of cannon balls stacked as though war would begin any day was a memorable experience.

During the summer of 1955, we took a trip back to Texas for a couple of weeks to visit family. Duane wanted to stay an extra week. Arrangements were made with Edna, Virgie's sister, for Duane to arrive in Haiti on the following Monday. As a twelve year old, Duane was eager to travel alone, with guidance from the airlines, we thought. However, we found the event to be different. Without our knowledge, Duane had boarded the plane in Houston; transferred in Atlanta; arrived in Miami, and boarded the plane to Port au Prince by himself, without any controlling help from the airlines. When he arrived at the Haiti terminal, the customs clearance, under the control of "Papa Doc" Duvallier, was pursued by Duane. Since he had learned Creole, he convinced Papa Doc to let him clear customs when Duane identified the compound location. Duane hired a taxi and came to our front door with his suitcase that Saturday. We were amazed at his travel process.

A Strange Breakfast

Trips to the island extremes were conditioned by church conventions or hurricane destruction surveillance. Hurricanes were annual events from June to November. On one trip to the western end of Haiti in 1955, I was the guest of one of our very remote church families. When I got up from my night of sleep on the straw bed, I was given a breakfast of goat chitterling soup. For those of you who don't know, chitterling is the small intestine. My problem was not in trying to be modest and pleasant to my host and his wife, but trying to chew on that intestine. It wouldn't respond like other foods I was used to eating. For lunch I was given the goat head cooked in full fashion with the jowls as the foremost item of the menu. To say the least, I learned what the term *missionary* meant from a brand-new perspective.

Building ten buildings on a fifteen-acre property became a big job. Trying to satisfy each missionary was a problem. The Beatys had taken a year off to finish an educational degree at Vanderbilt University in Nashville. Odine Morse had been the earliest missionary to Haiti, having arrived in the late '40s.

The Plot Thickens

As I stated in a previous chapter; "the complexities of life" became evident in 1955. Odine tried to persuade me to change my course of activity in the building program. Because I didn't build her home when she wished, it was reported in a scathing letter to the Mission's Board. Since I was appointed by the board, it was concluded that a review of the "Odine Letter" should be investigated. One Mission Board member was sent to Haiti to investigate and bring back his report for full board action. I gave a full verbal report which lasted until after 2 a.m. My position was expressed according to the issues. The board member sent to investigate was the brother of Odine—Raymond Morse. I had no idea what kind of action would be taken until I received a letter from Reverend Paul H. Walker, chairman of the Mission's Board and executive secretary for that department. Because of Raymond Morse's report, it was recommended that I was to be released from my authority as overseer of Haiti and only to be classified as the builder of the compound.

Here the plot thickens again. The complexities of the Haitian law strongly prohibit any person to be allowed to come to their island as a builder. My visa authority permitted me into their land specifically as a minister. This would be considered as taking away the privileges of the local native. When I informed Brother Walker that if he wished to enforce the board's decision of relieving me as a leader, I would thereby be compelled to resign my total authority and responsibility and leave Haiti when directed. The compound tasks were a full six months from being completed. Searching for another building authority might take a year or longer to replace me in this capacity.

A Positive Ending

The complexities go again from negative to positive. I received a new letter from Brother Walker. In speedy detail he stated, "From one German to another, you made your point." You will stay with your full authority until your job has been completed. Upon this decision, Odine decided to take a year off and get some sunshine in the good old U.S.A. Faye Singleton who was a missionary in the Dominican Republic came to be my secretary.

I finished my tasks in Haiti. I was happy that everything I had been assigned to do appeared successful. The growth of the church membership went from 7,500 at my arrival to 10,000. The number of churches expanded to 125. When I came back stateside and James Beaty returned to his new assignment in Haiti, a completed Bible School compound was built at a cost of $51,000. This beautiful compound was set to blossom with a mission ministry of instructing eager Haitians to become quality leaders for God.

During our three-year term in Haiti, we had the privilege of hosting and entertaining 103 visitors. At the beginning of this chapter, I described missions by touring the Caribbean countries.

One of the visitors who came to Haiti in March of 1956 was Basil Ellis, overseer of Missouri. I had known his brother, Vep, because of his prominence as a Gospel music writer. His brother, Henry, was on the Texas state council and helped select me as state youth director in 1951. But now I got acquainted with another one who, because of his visit and observance of my function in Haiti, was about to open a new door for me.

I was invited to come to Missouri to pastor. The church would be open with a change in pastors at the General Assembly of 1956. One reason for my appointment was because Brother Ellis was going to build a New Tabernacle and wanted me to be the engineer in completing its construction while he finished his last two-year term as overseer of Missouri. I was flabbergasted. I was to become the pastor of the Grand Avenue Church in St. Louis. It was the largest congregation west of the Mississippi at that time.

My assignment was completed in the spring of 1956. When we came home, it was with the feeling that a wonderful episode was now a part of our life story. The Missions Office was very highly expressive of our work. We were given contacts to speak at special events that summer. A schedule was made to visit the Phillips in Lexington. Brother Phillips had gone from Tremont to Kentucky as overseer in 1953. From Kentucky, we drove to Michigan to visit with the Spain Family. C. R. Spain was now the Michigan State Overseer. When I first met Brother Spain, he was one of the first four visitors to Haiti after our arrival December 31, 1953. The other three were L. C. Heaston, Estel Moore, and Floyd Timmerman. We reminisced about that first week with a lot of laughter.

I wonder if anybody would question whether God **was** and **is** in the arrangements? I was about to enter into a new venture of ministry wherein I would see that my life, my accomplishments, my destiny, and my future were totally within God's purview and control.

CHAPTER 12

GRAND AVENUE

*"The Spirit of the Lord is upon me,
because He hath anointed me to preach...."*
(Luke 4:18).

When Virgie and I arrived in the great city of Saint Louis, Missouri, in August of 1956, little did I realize that eight years of my future would unfold dramatically. A status of achievement that would happen reminded me that God multiplies the harvest if we preach the Word.

Grand Avenue Church had a vibrant congregation of worshipers. The Sunday school attendance was between 300 and 400 each week. One Easter we reached a record attendance of 575. I was always happy to see the eager people arrive to worship in that cathedral-style building at the corner of Grand Avenue at Forest Park. The strength and size was due to a strong bus ministry. The five buses would arrive at the Sunday school hour because of a very dedicated team of drivers who would spend hours before and after service to make this happen. Our church was just three miles from the downtown area, and only one-half mile from the University of St Louis. The hospital complex was a mile away. This was the hospital most sick would use because of its reputation. My visitation to pray with those who were ill always took the biggest portion of my workday.

Another Challenge

The primary reason for my assignment was based upon a condition of the departing previous pastor, R. E. Nuzum and his wife. They decided to return to Pennsylvania to be engaged in the nursing-home program of Sister Nuzum's family. Things did not work out with that move to their satisfaction. Twelve months later, they decided to return to St. Louis to minister in the city that had been their home for years. The problem was they had no pastorate to return to. They decided to go to the northern part of the city and start a new work. Their new members happened to be one-half of the Grand Avenue congregation.

The condition of dealing with a returning pastor whose intent was to build a position for his own future at the expense of dividing my congregation was not ideal. I devoted my efforts to expanding all activity to the support of my workers in the bus ministry. I then continued to minister in the pulpit and hospital ministry. Going to the Barnes Hospital, less than two miles away from where we lived, was an easy schedule.

The parsonage was on the second floor at 4372 Vista Avenue. This was the address of the old building where the congregation had begun decades earlier. The old church was an oblong box thirty-foot wide by seventy-foot long located on the corner of the block. The parsonage was on the second floor. Coming up the back stairway, the first room was the kitchen. The next room was the living room, and then the bedroom. Parallel to these three rooms were identical rooms that constituted the six-room parsonage. You may wonder why the kitchen was the first room accessed at the top of the back stairs. This was because it was above the lower level water system. Perhaps you wonder why I would identify this shabby layout here?

Having just completed a school complex in Haiti, the place where we resided was 1,500 feet elevation above sea level and three miles from the seacoast. Our panoramic view was the horizon to the west. It spread from left to right a distance of 35 miles with an island in the middle of the sea beyond Port-au-Prince.

I remind you here that I didn't accept this assignment because of its beauty. I was happy to labor in a location that had the largest Sunday school of any congregation west of the Mississippi at that time. The overseer believed that I could do the task of pastoral leadership and also help him in due process of time. I also had told the General Church authorities the reason for my desires. I had been asked by one of them if I would be willing to become the overseer of Montana at the next General Assembly. My response was that I felt I should first be a seasoned pastor. Little did I know at that time I would spend the next eight years in one of the loveliest municipal cities of America.

Activity in leadership was challenging. During my first year, the president of the Ladies Willing Worker Band approached me with this question: "Do you think you are old enough to pastor this big church?"

I said in response, "Sister, I am only thirty-two years old, but by the grace of God and His guidance, I think I can do it."

During the next year, when she said in a seedy reaction to a problem, "I resign," I responded with an okay. She later begged me to have her position back.

The conditions relating to the above paragraph was that since we were affected by the return of former Pastor

Nuzum, our congregation was only half its previous size. It was necessary for us to sell prepared lunches each week to the nearby commercial and industrial plants of the neighborhood. The financial budget still had the same obligations, but our income was insufficient to pay the mortgage on our lovely church. I was happy to deliver these lunches each week to the employees of Anhauser Busch Company, which was only a half-block away.

Learning to Play the Organ

I found the issues relevant to a split congregation were also problematic. I lost my organist and pianist to the new North St. Louis Church. I was musically inclined in that I could play the guitar and the accordion, but I was totally inept at how to play either the piano or organ. Our son, Duane, now twelve, had been a piano student since he was age seven. Being the pastor, I appointed him as our pianist. While he would make the rhythm, I would "hunt and peck" according to how I thought it should be on the organ. After all, who would tell me I shouldn't get some kind of musical value from the fabulous instrument on the platform. To say the least, I became proficient after long practice at the expense of a congregation who had no other alternative.

After two years, with a lot of prayer and preparation for the needs of a great congregation, we saw stability and growth. Leadership change of our state overseer brought Reverend Paul Stallings to Missouri. I was elected to the State Council and was able to find out how wonderful was the "Show Me State," better known as Missouri. Living in the old parsonage at 4372 Vista Avenue became history after three years. The church officials authorized us to get a new place to call home. That location was three miles south of the church at 3924 Meramac Street in South St. Louis. We found the location pleasant and better than the previous dwelling.

The Famous Eight

The First World Pentecostal Conference was held in Jerusalem in 1961. My overseer, Paul Stallings, influenced me to join him and six others on a thirty-day venture. The group included Charles Conn, Lewis Willis, both from the Publishing Department; Cecil Knight, and Don Aultman, from the General Youth Department; Floyd Timmerman and Paul Stallings, state overseers; and Estel Moore and I, local pastors. Our journey began on the renowned ship SS United States. For five days most of us enjoyed our travel, except Floyd Timmerman, who was seasick the five days we were crossing the Atlantic.

Excitement prevailed as we saw the famous places of London, Paris, Zurick, Munich, Florence, Rome, and Athens—seven famous cities of Europe. We traveled the European Continent by train. This type of travel across Europe was a great experience.

At that time, the status of Israel was of unsettled war conditions throughout their territory. While in the King David Hotel outside of Jerusalem, I could see and hear the sounds of war activity. We had to go across steel road-barriers to get to our hotel in Jerusalem. It was there I discovered that I had forgotten my Bible at the King David Hotel. Since I had crossed the barriers and my passport had been stamped by Israel, it was impossible for me to return to an Arab country. I was fortunate to have an Embassy official bring my Bible to me.

We went to Egypt after the Jerusalem conference. To see the great city of Cairo, the Sphinx, and the Pyramids made me excited to know that I had come to the world-famous territory where Moses lived 2000-plus years before Christ. We saw the mummies and relics of 4,000 years in time before our eyes.

Traveling homeward brought the eight of us back through Athens, Greece. Because I had a brother, David, who was stationed in Asia Minor in the Air Force, I made contact with him and we spent time together in Greece. Visiting the Acropolis in Athens and the Corinthian location in the lower peninsula of Greece was a Biblical re-creation of that great church at Corinth made famous by Paul's Epistle to the Corinthians.

After thirty days, we arrived home via air travel. My mind revels today in remembering such famous places with this group called "The Famous Eight." I will always cherish this time as it relates to life. I have been blessed.

Mistaken Identity

Pastoral duties are basically routine. I had the pleasure of serving our church families in every capacity. One event was extraordinary. A local couple came to me late one afternoon. Her brother, a vagabond type, was always being apprehended by the police for his problematic lifestyle. He typically slept under the overpass or bridge nearby. He was also classified as a beggar, seeking a hand-out whenever or wherever one could be obtained.

I was told that Mary's brother had an accident and had died. He was in the morgue and needed to be identified and arrangements for the funeral. I was asked to go with her. When we arrived, the review began. Every mark that was observed showed the scar on his forehead, the one on his arm, his size, and his features were all defined. The one question Mary asked the morgue attendant, a Negro, was as follows: "My brother had blue eyes, this man's eyes are brown. Do they change colors when they die?"

"I guess so," he said. The body was claimed, sent to the funeral home for preparation, and we had a private ceremonial burial of John. His body was taken to the family plot, and we gave the family our best effort to comfort their loss.

Ten days later, the police department contacted me. The I. D. report of the victim had been dispatched to verify his fingerprints. The report came back that the dead man's fingerprints belonged to a person from Louisville, Kentucky. That family had notified the police, who then notified me that I had buried the wrong man. The results were perplexing. Now what? The dead man's family told the police that they did not intend to dig up the grave. The case was "closed." What next?

John showed up at church the next Sunday with a smile on his face. He was always sharing his smile. His comments were, "Pastor, I came back." He had been recuperating from a drug overdose at an Illinois recovery location some thirty miles from St. Louis.

The church was an easy congregation to lead after four years. The people were respectful and cooperative under all circumstances. When we took our vacation one year to Florida, we were invited to share our schedule with our friends, Brother and Sister Phillips. They had fulfilled their time in Kentucky and were finishing four years in Florida as the overseer. All indications projected that A. M. Phillips would be elected to the Executive Committee.

Sure enough when August and General Assembly time came, He was elevated to that position.

A New Chapter

In 1962 the World Mission Board became a new chapter in my life. L. H. Aultman was director of World Missions. W. E Johnson was board chair. Board members during the four years of my tenure were Elmo Jennings, D. A, Biggs, T. L. Forester, H. B. Ramsey, P. H. McCarn, Estel D. Moore, Hershel Diffie, and me. James L. Slay came to the Mission Department as the international representative. Vessie D. Hargrave became the executive missions director, replacing L. H. Aultman in 1964. It was a feeling of ecstasy for me to have such a status with these ministers.

The next month, C. R. Spain, general secretary, asked me to go with him to the Iowa minister's meeting. He flew to St. Louis and we drove to Iowa for that meeting. This began a very favorable association with the church leadership over many years. Brother Spain had come to Haiti the first week after we arrived there.

A little over one year later, while serving on the mission's board, events focused on board action to develop an upgrade to the mission policy. By being part of the committee, I could see that a better policy was needed to help control appointments, tenure, salary, and all related issues to keep the system balanced.

In further review, we recognized a need to keep our funds solvent where possible. We had $50,000 surplus above operational funds. A motion prevailed by the board that we invest these funds. The local banker called the department to ask if there was any objection to loaning our funds to two of our own ministers? Their project was to improve a local motel they owned on South Lee Highway in Cleveland. Approval was given.

Here the issues get complex. I had not, heretofore, ever given much reasoning to how or if politics would be a part of my experiences as it related to my church activity or assignments. I had long believed that God had placed leadership at the head of the organization through His purpose and will. Because Christ is the head of the Church, I accepted relevance in leadership and operation to be God-ordained, because the person serving God was under His jurisdiction and will.

A Complex Issue

Years earlier, in B. T. S., I learned the principle of church hierarchy. I learned that our organization operated under the Episcopal system, having a polity where the bishops were the authority. I concluded that not only was this a Biblical precept, but it was the way any church organization should function.

When the general overseer gave direction that our investment of helping two of our church friends in their personal loan needs was illegal, we scrambled to correct the issue. The problem was that our investment was in the form of a second mortgage loan. Church policy regulation declared any loan must be controlled by a first mortgage. E. C. Thomas and Lewis Willis, owners of that Diplomat Motel, had every right to own any property they chose. What made this issue complex was that our invested funds were being used to put in a swimming pool. Our Mission Department funds were being appropriated by Mr. Banker to expedite this operation.

Since church policy prohibited its members from mixed bathing as one of its rules, the "fat was in the fire." I was asked by the board to act as the arbitrator to resolve this crisis. We met together with all parties and finally received funds from Thomas and Willis to resolve the second mortgage loan. Our funds were back in our mission's fund account. However, since L. H. Aultman was deemed to be eligible to be promoted, through election at the General Assembly, his "Political coattail" was dirty. When the General Assembly election was final, L. H. Aultman had been given the political shaft and Vessie D. Hargraves was elected to fill Aultman's position.

A New Location

Our church was prominent in that it was at a location of two primary streets of the city, which was directly in the route of the projected interstate highway that was to be built traversing midtown St. Louis. We were now required to begin looking for a new location for our congregation.

The complexity of this situation was not that it should be interpreted as an adversity for me personally, but I knew that to move a congregation from the roots of its neighborhood to a distant location, would affect the size of our attendance in time. However, there was no alternative. The interstate highway would be built and our location was in the direct location of the road. If we did not find a location, buy the land, and build a new facility for worship, our church would be dead.

Together the leadership and the congregation authorized a committee to find a place. The first condition was that it be accessible for everyone. The second reference was that it be on a primary road. The third condition was that it not be too close to an existing congregation so as to affect them. The fourth condition was that we not move to the edge of the city, and, thereby be out of touch with our people.

St. Louis is located at the confluence of the Missouri River where it enters the Mississippi River; therefore, we were bound by an east and north parameter. To consider east of our location would put us downtown. To go north, we would have to cross the Missouri River. Subsequently, it was either south or west. To go south would place us in subdivisions of questionable conditions and access. The only other option was to go west. West by northwest was industrial and near the airport. The last option was to head southwest. Ten miles southwest of our lovely Grand Avenue was the Webster Groves community. We located a five-acre parcel of land on Big Bend Boulevard at W. Glendale Avenue.

It became necessary for us as a church to obtain a qualified architect to provide us with proper specifications that would pass all building codes in the city of Webster Groves. This turned out to be a blessing because we were able to accept the details of the proposed buildings of the church sanctuary and the nearby parsonage without conflict to any or all authorities involved.

The difficulties were that because of the tight specifications of code compliance, our financial limitation was set at $125,000 for the total project. In due course of time, because of my building knowledge, I was required to reduce the proposed architectural plans and only provide a limited Sunday school class space when we ran out of money. I completed the building project in two years and was pastor of our congregation at that location almost four years. The dedication of this marvelous property was conducted by Dr. Wade H. Horton in the spring of 1964.

This facility was beautiful because the competent architect gave the church a landmark design. For the next thirty years that location was the lighthouse for souls. When it became necessary to expand property size, due to land limitation, because of its wonderful location and high design, it was sold for three quarters of $1 million.

I finished eight wonderful years of my ministry in the City of St. Louis. It was time to move.

At the General Assembly of 1964, my recognition as a leader seemed to position me for consideration of an assignment as state overseer. I had declined the status eight years earlier because I felt I needed to have experience as a competent pastor before I should try to lead other pastors. At Dallas I was approached by one of the Executive Committee who asked if I would consider going to Oregon as overseer. I gave an affirmative response. The appointment, of course, was conditioned upon the majority of the Executive Committee's approval. I could not know if I would be appointed by the new committee or not. As the events of the week unfolded, I learned that the committee chose to place Frank Culpepper in that state. The state of Washington was open and the committee placed M. H. Kennedy as the new overseer of that state. It was not openly identified, but I recognized that the general overseer was more inclined to appoint Kennedy than me. Even though Horton had dedicated my sanctuary in recent weeks, he had known Kennedy for years since serving as overseer of Mississippi for four years. Having left that state to become general overseer, Horton was cognizant of Kennedy's twenty-year term as pastor of Bailey

Avenue church in Jackson. I was then asked to become the pastor at Jackson, Mississippi. The reasons given me by the committee were because Kennedy had outgrown his old building, he declared that he was not competent to build a sanctuary that had been approved by the congregation. Kennedy's previous additions to his old building was evidence that he was not a builder of elegant sanctuaries. The final result of my new assignment—I was going to Bailey Avenue to pastor a great church and build a new sanctuary and Sunday school property.

The circumstances that prevailed in my appointments in the church were mind-boggling to me. In 1951, I instantly was appointed youth director in Texas, because the overseer needed an engineer to construct a building on the new Texas Campground. In 1952, I was sent to South Carolina and became the assistant pastor of the largest church, at that time, in our organization. In 1954, I was sent to Haiti. The previous chapter tells my story in full detail. In 1956, I came to St. Louis. This chapter tells my story. Now in 1964, I am about to engage in a phase of activity and ministry almost beyond definition.

We arrived in Jackson, Mississippi, in August of 1964. Ruth, Mississippi, was Virgie's birthplace. Her father, W.F. Ainsworth, began his ministry in Mississippi more than thirty years earlier. Virgie felt like she was returning home. Many of her kinfolk lived less than fifty miles away. The Bailey Avenue church was the largest congregation in Mississippi. I recognized that I was being assigned to a special work in an area noted as the most reactionary state in the nation as it related to imbalance between black and white cultures. Having served in Haiti, I had developed a broad acceptance about how to treat this cultural crisis. I went to Jackson at the height of U. S. reaction nationwide on this subject. How did things work out?

CHAPTER 13

EXTREME CIRCUMSTANCES

"Let love be without dissimulation"
(Romans 12:9)

The Bailey Avenue Church in Jackson, the capital city of Mississippi, had a strong pattern of activity as it related to their style of worship. The pastor had been their leader for twenty years, Brother M. H. Kennedy, was a great preacher and a good man. I had not known him or his family prior to my appointment to the church. My new overseer was T. L Forrester. He and I had worked side by side the previous two years on the World Mission's Board. I was delighted to be working with an overseer whom I highly respected as my new leader.

The church was a vibrant congregation of people of middle-class status. They were not to be considered as poverty type, nor socially high class. While a few had higher education, as a whole, they should be noted generally as even being tempered and balanced.

Extreme Conditions

The church was established decades earlier at the border of the city limits. The population of the church was totally white. The movement of the black community ultimately bordered the church vicinity. With the cultural ethics of the nation in the decade of the 1960 era, the city of Jackson and its environs was a bomb ready to explode at any time. Environmentally, the complex social and cultural conditions affecting the nature of an individual or community was boiling. The whole state was affected by interaction between The Continental North and South as it related to the African-American culture.

The church accepted us as a family with open arms. Duane and I sang and played the piano and organ for our own accompaniment. We adapted to the needs of the church. The previous pastor's preaching style was not mine. I didn't jump and shout like he did, nor was Virgie's short hair in compliance with the code of ethics of the radical conservative division of this church congregation. This church was inclined to enforce the church rules and regulations relating to external appearance.

The positive emphasis from this congregation was the fact that the church had grown and needed a new building. Brother Kennedy had added to buildings at other times with what I would call an add-on to an add-on. They had come to the place where there could not be a further add-on. The church owned a large frontage of property on Bailey Avenue. It was one block in length on this street, but twenty years of growth of the church and the simple frame structure of the previous building necessitated a new type and style for the future. This became the final reason for Kennedy's new assignment and relocating.

The congregation had been fully informed by the Executive Committee of the church of my past eight-year tenure and history of building at Grand Avenue and Webster Groves. Therefore, I was welcomed with open arms relating to the goals of their new building. The plan specifications and city code compliance relating to the building were obtained in swift order.

A large "A" Frame Truss-type interior was the design of the new building. This was similar to the type I had constructed three years earlier at Webster Groves. The auditorium was designed to seat 400 people. Adjacent to the new sanctuary was the Sunday school area that fit between the old and new buildings. It took just over a year to complete the structure.

Family Issues

After twelve months in a wonderful mood with a great congregation, I heard a story about Virgie's family that shook me up. W.F Ainsworth, Virgie's father, had spent all his life starting as a young teenager in ministry. It seemed to him that he should retire from the heavy load of being pastor. He had been in Mississippi, Louisiana, Arkansas, and Texas preaching for over forty-five years. His thinking about theology motivated him to leave the organization in 1943. He came back into the Church of God two years later. The church regulations mandated that to obtain a pension at retirement, one must have twenty years of unbroken service. When it was determined that he had only nineteen years since his return, he found it unfortunate that he would have no pension, but because of bad health he could not carry on.

His son, my brother-in-law, Bill Ainsworth, accepted the church in Pasadena, Texas. This church had great growth under the competent ministry of W. F. Ainsworth. Bill was soon expanding the church in its growth. However, his father moved into a small twenty-four by twenty-four, cracker-box shanty. This was all he could obtain with the funds in his bank account. I was so affected that I traveled from Jackson to Pasadena frequently to try to comfort a distressed minister.

Concurrently my parents, Henry and Thelma Heil, were at a crisis in their retirement years. Dad had retired from business in 1960. He had reached retirement at age 65 and was accepting that wonderful Social Security check to aid him in enjoying his future. Unfortunately, Dad's fiscal resources were not sufficient to sustain the requirements of survival on the income he received from Uncle Sam.

Dad obtained a 140-acre plot on State Highway 75, across the road from one of my brothers. A. C. (Punk) and Mickey had moved to Buffalo, 125 miles from Houston in 1954. Punk and Mickey had become successful cattle farmers, as well as growing watermelons on their ranch. Property was cheap in Buffalo when they purchased this property in 1954. At $5 per acre, they bought a square mile—640 acres.

Dad found it impossible to sustain his budget because he was unable to find employment at age sixty-nine. He decided to sell his property and get out from under his financial burden.

When I heard of my father-in-law's plight, and hearing of my dad's similar predicament, I determined to find a way to help me obtain a stable future without having to depend on the church with their meager pension plan for my future.

Upon negotiating with Dad for the purchase of his property, I calculated the costs of sustaining Dad's Farmers Home Loan mortgage and the price to pay off the loan on the contract I negotiated with Mom and Dad. I went to the bank in Jackson and borrowed $7,500. I now had three obligations to sustain—Dad's home loan first mortgage, Dad's second mortgage for his equity, and my unsecured bank loan payment. I was determined at age forty-one that I would not be victimized with my destiny as a retired minister—65 years old or more—without a place to call home after my parsonage days were over.

It took me fifteen years to pay off that Jackson bank loan and Dad's equity loan. I negotiated further with Mom and Dad to allow them to buy back the house with one acre that they called home, with the stipulation that I would be the only one to buy it back when they died.

A Crisis of 'Color'

Now things seemed to be following the plan of routine activity. The church was growing. Everything seemed to be going well until the nationwide flames of violence of 1964-65 corrupted the culture of the American Negro and their fight for acceptable recognition. These issues were fanned to an explosion in Mississippi. People who had lived a jittery life, relating to this situation, were always on edge about how to act when it became a public issue. The same could be said about our local congregation. It was a constant question about whether this kind of crisis might happen within our church's four walls.

When the discussion arose in late 1965 about what to do or how to react if Blacks should come to the church, I was asked, "As pastor, what will you do?" Having grown up in the North, and lived in the South, I had known the variation of cultural acceptance and reaction to rejection about these issues, and I had a broad concept and openness to them. Also, I had spent three years in Haiti. That nation, totally Black, had received me with open arms. Even though as a white leader, I had all of my functions with them on an open basis, I never did anything that would place me on a superior level. I shared this with my

Bailey Avenue Council. Then a question was posed by the council:"Will you allow Blacks to come in to worship?" When my remarks were explained openly, as I state them here in this writing, things got quiet.

The council did not become openly severe, but undercover, it became evident that things were about to explode. The male group of the church was radically inclined to enforce the nonwhite/nonattendance in any of our services. One Sunday, even though it was comfortably warm, a person arrived at the service wearing an overcoat. He sat near the backdoor. It was never openly defined, but it was alleged that he had a pistol in his coat pocket. His hands remained in his coat during the entire worship service.

The next two months were strictly "itchy." What do I do if the Black worshiper attempts to enter the front door?

The next thing I knew, I was being notified by my state overseer that I was being requested to leave my church and be reassigned. Brother Forrester was a very easy-going person. He and his family had welcomed us with open-arms eighteen months earlier. We had pleasant personal contacts as close friends. Now to be informed by him that we were going to be moved, I asked why? Brother Forrester informed me that the general overseer had advised him to take action to move me. This upset me. It was devastating to Virgie. What had we done wrong?

When the time came for the church conference on that Sunday afternoon, we were all seated and awaiting the verdict. The state overseer had concluded that the order from above to replace me would be accepted. What came to light in that same conference was that the local church was being asked to approve the new pastor being submitted via general overseer's order. The new appointee was the famed minister, the Reverend J. T. Roberts.

Brother Roberts had been a famous leader in the Church of God for decades. He had served as the National African-American Overseer of that group from 1958 to 1965. Because of a fiduciary problem in serving as the overseer of the African-American group in the northeast part of our nation, Roberts was being transferred somewhere to calm that situation. The odd part of this equation is that the local congregation rejected the general office's recommendation that he become the pastor for Bailey Avenue.

New Destination—Maryland

We were advised to pack and move to Salisbury, Maryland. This congregation was a famous church where Raymond Crowley had been their leader. We began our preparation for moving. In the meantime, the Mission Board schedule was approaching. I went to that board meeting with a lot of apprehension. I wondered how I should approach the general overseer?

Having spent one month in travel and fellowship in 1961 on our Pentecostal World Conference with the "Famous Eight," one of whom was Charles Conn, I went first to the office of the Assistant General Overseer Charles Conn. After explaining the issues to Brother Conn as I perceived them, I heard him say, "Wayne, you can win the battle and lose the war."

I went from there to the office of the general overseer. In order to show the rationale of things that were to happen in that meeting, I digress to a previous timeframe.

Wade Horton became the state overseer of Mississippi in 1956. He served as Mississippi Overseer four years.

He was well received and famous for his stance in spiritual pomposity. When M. H. Kennedy was appointed to the state of Washington four years later, it was common discussion in our local church council meetings that telephone calls were regularly received. James Kennedy, brother to M.H. was chair of the local church board. We knew that M. H. had an interest on how things were going. After all, M. H. was pastor for twenty years. It is my assumption that James Kennedy kept his brother well informed, and that M. H kept his brother well advised.

When I asked Brother Horton why I was compelled to leave Bailey Avenue, he said, "According to the information I received, you had done nothing."

I was shocked! I asked him, "From where did you get this information?"

His remarks were, "From Jamie" (James Kennedy).

I said to Brother Horton, "In the past eighteen months, our congregation has grown twenty-five percent and increased financially by that same amount. Furthermore, I have built a fabulous new sanctuary and school complex on that same block where the old building stood."

Salisbury

Brother Horton said, "I didn't know that." It was now too late to reverse decisions. I was on my way to a place called "The Famous Eastern Shore of Maryland."

When we arrived in Salisbury in the spring of 1966, the events of packing, moving, unpacking, and coping with the emotional conditions of the previous two months were devastating. Not only was I apprehensive of how I would adapt to my assignment, but I was perplexed on what to do for Virgie. As a fabulous companion, she never complained about anything relating to her health. I vividly recalled every day of how Virgie, because of her heart problems, was compelled to spend two hours of every day taking a nap in the afternoon to be able to make her day.

Now in a matter of weeks, that episode which never left her memory, "You must have surgery before age forty-five or you will die," became an edict. The surgeon who advised us said; "It is not a matter of *when*, but *where*."

As stated in an earlier chapter, the reports of the Maryland doctors were accepted by Dr. Michael DeBakey in Houston. In the first few weeks of our residency in Maryland, we were trying to keep life from ending for Virgie.

Virgie survived. Because of the famous Houston doctor and the blessed help from a wonderful God who knew all about our future, we continued to trust in Him. That scripture by the Psalmist David is so emphatic that I choose to write it in its totality. Psalms 103:1-5: "Bless the Lord, O my soul, and all that is within me, bless his holy name. Bless the Lord, O my soul, and forget not all his benefits. Who forgiveth all thine iniquities; who healeth all thy diseases: Who redeemeth thy life from destruction; who crowneth thee with lovingkindness and tender mercies; Who satisfieth thy mouth with good things; so that thy youth shall be renewed like the eagle's."

Virgie became vibrant for the next six weeks due to this wonderful operation. Then a problem, unknown at the beginning, surfaced. She had been given a blood transfusion during surgery that was contaminated. She had hepatitis C.

Having moved to Salisbury in early 1966, the church was soon to vote for a pastor for the ensuing two-year term. We were pleased to learn from Maryland State Overseer,

Tom W. Day, that we had received a 95 percent vote. This indicated that even though we were new to the congregation, we had been accepted. The overseer informed us that the 5 percent vote was given to the previous pastor who had been appointed to another state. Therefore, it was his conclusion that we could consider it a 100 percent approval to remain for the ensuing two years.

The transition to Maryland brought us in close proximity to Duane and Carol who had been working as music ministers for Henry Ellis in Newport News, Virginia. During their time in Virginia, Caresa Dawn was born January 27, 1966. The closeness to us motivated them to want to move to be near us. Subsequently, they were appointed to fill the same role with us as they had with Henry Ellis. Duane filled his position well. Carol applied for and received a job with the telephone company. She was happy to be serving in this capacity.

Again the issue of position and acceptance by anyone or everybody came into question. The references that are stated here are not previously recorded on paper but were transmitted to me verbally, and off the record officially, due to Carol's job status. It was in her job location that she overheard the conversation between parties on the phone system. What she heard was overwhelming. The Salisbury church clerk, in a phone conversation to the state overseer, Tom Day, was heard by Carol to say, "We need a change in pastor for our church. He doesn't fit here on the Eastern Shore; he's a foreigner, and besides that, he's got a sick wife."

Brother Day was a very personal friend of mine. He was a brother-in-law to my previous overseer, Paul Stallings. Working in Maryland was not a problem for me.

After all, I didn't ask to be sent to Salisbury. It was by appointment from the office of the general overseer.

It is now near General Assembly time and Tom Day asked me what I wished to do. I was, first of all, perplexed. I did not choose my last move. Neither did I want to act defensively to try to prove my competence. Furthermore, Virgie was reacting to her blood complications from surgery. As a response to Tom I asked, "What do you want me to do?"

His response was very open. "You can stay here and fight for your position," he said, "or I can move you, with your approval to another church." I responded by saying that I would leave my assignment to my overseer.

Overseer Day said the pastor of the very large church in Alexandria, Virginia, will be open at the General Assembly. Frank W. Lemmons is retiring and the church will be available. My reaction was uncertain. My comments opened the door to an alternative. I told Tom that if I made the decision based upon size and prestige, it may or may not be God's will. All my life I had conditioned my thinking that my assignments or church appointments were God-ordained by the authority of those over me in the Lord. If I choose my destination for relocating; would it be God's will? I was then informed that the Ferndale, Michigan, church could be my next appointment. Tom's brother, Ralph, would like to move to Maryland and work under his brother. I told Tom that I would not select my future assignment, but would leave it to him to make the decision and the appointment. Because Virgie was not capable of doing what she wished to do as a pastor's wife, she chose to leave the future to my discretion.

More Changes

The events of the previous two years were hard to define, hard to defend, and very hard to accept. I had come a long way from the young sixteen year old who started preaching in Texas. My experiences then were of a happy young man who believed God had called him, and who was willing to undergo or endure any episode in the ministry. My experiences now had me questioning, *where is God in these events*? I knew then as I know now, God is still the Almighty, Omnipresent, Omniscient Being. Even though I believed that the move from Jackson to Salisbury was political and what transpired during these two years was unfair, I still believe that my God did not abandon or forsake me. Neither did I leave the ministry; I considered everything in this matter to be a very political maneuver to advance someone else.

In 1996 at the Alabama Prayer Conference Billy Chalk gave me a new revelation. Billy Chalk was the Sunday school superintendent, the worship song leader, as well as a board member of the local church at Jackson. His Brother, Elton Chalk, also was a leader and board member. These two brothers were very much associated with "Jamie" Kennedy because of their long-term friendship when M. H. Kennedy was pastor. Billy reported to me the total story of that 1966 political maneuver.

The Chalk family had moved from Mississippi because their son, David, had become a medical doctor and was practicing in Anniston, Alabama. With residency in Alabama, it was a normal thing for a family of his caliber to be present at any state meeting. When Billy met me at that Mobile, Alabama, meeting, he expressed extreme apology to me. His references expanded on all the facts of my dismissal. Then he expressed that I did the Jackson, Bailey Avenue Church the best work that had been done. He expressed over and over how very sorry he was for having been involved in the council as he was to adversely affect me.

A very rare incident follows. This is a small footnote by way of sharing this paragraph within this chapter. The widow of Paul Barker, Gladys, stated that they were given the same treatment. They followed me as pastor six years after I left and were emphatically told that no Blacks were to be allowed in a church service. What a coincidence. This statement was shared with us at a restaurant in Cleveland, Tennessee, the same day that I am writing this chapter in 2012.

CHAPTER 14

BACK NORTH

"Be instant in season...."
(2 Timothy 4:2).

In 1939 I moved from the frigid state of South Dakota. As a child I rejoiced when leaving the north because I was escaping this freezing kind of winter. I was so happy that my parents had chosen to make the South our home. Now twenty seven-years later, August 1966, I am back in the cold winter zone again. I find myself in the north central United States. This vicinity in church work proved to be fabulous. Michigan is a wonderful area that I had not previously known. I was about to enter into a venture that I could not fathom.

The state of Michigan is in a class as no other. My mother had come from the state of Minnesota, "A land of 10,000 lakes." When I noted the references about Michigan, I learned that the state boasted it was "A State of 11,037 inland lakes." Also, four of the five Great Lakes of America border Michigan. They are Lake Erie, Lake Huron, Lake Michigan, and Lake Superior. I also found that the winter temperature was similar to South Dakota with three months of the year always averaging below the freezing zone. As a child, I rejoiced when leaving the North about escaping this kind of winter. I now moved into the cold winter zone again.

A Life-Changing Event

Life for Virgie and me had been topsy-turvy for the previous six months. Not everything had gone well. We had been adversely affected by church-related events from the Bailey Avenue political push against our survival there. We were ordered by the general overseer's directive to move to Salisbury, Maryland. This event affected Virgie so much that she was compelled to undergo the heart surgery her doctor had predicted years earlier. Now Virgie had gone through a life-changing event. However, open-heart surgery had given us a new hope. Not everything had gone well. A bad blood transfusion during surgery affected her recovery. The Salisbury church clerk's manipulation against us because of Virgie's health and my being called a "foreigner" because I was not from Maryland's Eastern Shore, made my destiny unsure. I had to consider an adjustment in my work schedule.

During the past ten years, I had been going full speed as pastor of three different churches that averaged over 250 per service twelve months of the year. Do I keep going at that pace? I concluded that whatever assignment was given to me by my overseer that I would accept it as God's will.

A church in the Washington D. C. area was available, also Ferndale, Michigan. My Maryland overseer, Tom Day, appointed me to the Michigan church. Tom Day's brother, Ralph Day, had been a long-term pastor at Ferndale. However, Ralph's style of leadership became unacceptable to Ferndale. Although the declared membership was equal to my previous assignments, the Sunday attendance had dropped to fifty at preaching time. Ralph had a penchant for holding service on Sunday until after one o'clock. This became unacceptable to the Ferndale group.

The Ferndale Church

Our new place to live and work was Ferndale, bordering Detroit on the north. One week after our arrival, I had to put Virgie back in the hospital. Because of a bad blood transfusion during her heart surgery, she had contracted hepatitis. What should we do? The doctors advised us the bad blood had to be corrected. To summarize this part of her situation, I quote the doctors references. Her liver had sustained damage from hepatitis to the extent of fifty-nine percent of loss of her liver. Her prognosis by the doctor was good and that this event was to be nearly a two-year time span for her recovery. The conditions of her bad health and slow recovery made it my obligation to be a "special caregiver" to Virgie, which was almost a full-time task. My question was: "How do I fulfill my church responsibility?"

One of the blessings became evident when a lady member of the church came to me. She was the wife of Reverend F. B. Koshewitz. They were pastors at Ferndale many years earlier. She said, "I was sick for two years and they did not require my husband to respond to any calls. Instead, he was told to take care of my needs." Brother and Sister Koshewitz were at the time of this conversation members at Ferndale. It became evident that the congregation was willing to accept my wife's sickness as my responsibility to bring her back to good health. I found my moods and feelings completely at ease. Also, God knew and He would help us survive and respond to all the church needs in due time.

It was a wonderful association to have Reverend Estel D. Moore as my overseer. He and I were buddies together when the "famous eight" went to Jerusalem five years earlier. He and Evelyn, his wife, were very special friends for the next four years when we worked under his leadership. He was also one of the first four ministers to visit us in Haiti in 1953. The thirteen-year period since our Haiti acquaintance brought us together many times. He and I also served on the World Mission's Board together. What a blessing to feel comfortable about what I would do without wondering if I was under scrutiny.

Brother Moore was no stranger to Michigan. He was pastor of the West Flint Church when we traveled to Jerusalem in 1961. As the newly appointed overseer in Michigan, he was able to act with good knowledge about the needs and goals of the state.

Another Building Project

Typically after the General Assembly, the next month brings the ministers of the state together to plan for their programs and work for the new church year. It might have been coincidence, but immediate plans for the campground involved building some cottages across the lake from the tabernacle. Because of Estel's knowledge of my activity in building, he assigned me as supervisor of the campground.

Eight cottages were built that first year. Maintaining the property was routine. However, the next spring, we had an excessive rainfall and the lake could not contain the flood. The overflow pipe that was supposed to maintain and control the water level became clogged by trash. I saw the water begin its action on the gravel road that constituted the dam for the lake. It was trickling down the back side of the dam. Soon the grass gave way to the erosive reaction to the water flowing down twenty feet from the top of the road to the valley below and it took its toll. In less than two hours, the dirt of the dam opened a cavity and water began a turbulent downfall. Soon the road began to crumble from the water turbulence. A twenty-foot wide opening in the dam brought the calamity to its finish. For many weeks, I had to oversee the task of rebuilding the dam.

Camp meeting was always a time of blessing. I have been in these kinds of services since I was ten years old, beginning in North Dakota in 1935. Since that time, I have had the spiritual excitement of camp-meeting worship on campgrounds in Texas, Pennsylvania, South Carolina, Arkansas, Missouri, Kansas, Washington, Oregon, Mississippi, Maryland, Michigan, Wisconsin, Hawaii, New Jersey, New York, Indiana, Illinois, West Virginia, Alabama, and Tennessee. These events happened when I was either a pastor or an invited guest. With these twenty different locations, I found my spiritual development at camp meeting to be a blessing beyond definition.

Being musically involved since early childhood, I was always a part of the music portion of a service. Since St. Louis days, I had learned to play the organ. Organ music was a prominent portion of the music program at that time. Now in Michigan, I became one of the musicians at camp meeting. This gave me recognition among the ministerial group, as well as with the congregation. I was immediately treated by all as long-time friends. By the end of the year, I was elected to the state council.

The Ferndale Church was a highly respected church. It had some prominent leaders in the past. Elmo and Dorothy Jennings had been pastor years before. Elmo was on the General Mission's Board during my tenure on that board. Because his two daughters married while they were in Ferndale, those daughters were continuing residents even though the parents had moved to Washington D. C. and then to the Bahamas. I had the privilege of preaching for Elmo while they were in Nassau. I also had special friendship with his two sons-in-law, Delbert Rose and Harold Woods. Delbert was a pastor in Michigan and Harold was a prominent person on the National Layman's Board.

A New Policy

The Ferndale church stabilized in its attendance and grew to where they wanted to expand by relocating and building on new property. I began to pursue the possibility of a loan, but the banker stated that the church trustees did not have financial capability to permit the creating of a mortgage. However, I was advised of a different procedure to obtain the funds necessary to get the church relocated. The general church polity did not exist to allow this new process. It was necessary to go into a totally new procedure. With this new knowledge from the bank, I wrote to headquarters to General Overseer Ray Hughes and gave him a letter to define this new process. After pursuing the matter with the Executive Council, it was approved to submit the proposal to the Minister's Council during the General Assembly. The proposed new polity, if and when it became law, would apply to local, state, and general by-laws of the church. Up until this time (1968), all loans for mortgages had to have the trustees sign the loan papers and they, individually, were liable for any mortgage loan when in default. Therefore, it was virtually impossible to obtain large mortgage loans.

The specific word that applied to the proposed new law was the word *hypothecate*. The meaning of this word is "to pledge (property) as security to a creditor without transfer of title or possession—to mortgage." This motion came to the floor during the 1968 General Assembly Minister's Council. It was so unusual that I was the only one who spoke to the motion. It was submitted to the floor as three different motions because it related to three different levels—local, state, and general. No other person spoke for or against the motions. When the moderator, Ray Hughes, called for a vote, each level was passed without any objection. In other words, the total proposal passed 100 percent. It also passed the General Assembly vote without objection. After the sessions concluded, I was greeted with a synonym surname: "Hypothecate Heil." This identity was branded on my reputation from that year and for many decades to come by friends who really knew me.

What is wonderful about this new law in church polity is that loans are now able to be secured. Local church loans, state -level loans, and general church loans are available if and when it is certified that the financial status of the borrower is within their loan eligibility.

The local church was very good to us. I was able to build back a stable attendance at worship time. The concept of enlarging the Ferndale building was not practical. The church lot was not capable of allowing an expansion. We did not find it feasible to relocate to another township while I was pastor. The church eventually did relocate to Madison Heights. They obtained a large tract of land and did a great improvement to their status.

A Second Open-Heart Surgery

During the end of the second year, doctors' reports indicated Virgie had severe problems. The valve that had been placed in her heart was called a "Star-Edwards Valve." It was a one-inch metal ring with two u-shaped rings attached. Inside this ring was a small plastic ball that functioned like a pump when the blood pressure came through her mitral valve in her heart. This ring was sown inside of her heart to make it function as the flesh-mitral-valve is supposed to do. Four sutures of the sixteen that held this valve had broken loose from the heart flesh. She was admitted to the hospital in Houston for another open-heart surgery.

Dr. Debakey greeted us when we arrived that August day of 1968. He performed the operation very professionally and informed us of all the details. He had remembered us since it was only two years since Virgie's first surgery. At this time, I opened up a dialogue with him. I expressed the conditions that prevail when a pastor shares the moments of a parishioner's passing. I asked Dr. DeBakey a very pointed question: "Can I watch you perform surgery on a patient? I have watched many people die. I would like to see how a surgeon helps people live."

Dr. DeBakey said, "Sure. Make contact with my associate who will give you a pass to the surgery section and you can see me, along with other apprentices from the second-floor observation section."

The next day I was permitted into the surgery section. The area for viewing was a four-section location. When one group of doctors and nurses work at their section of the room, there are three more similar areas for simultaneous functions. For six hours I went from section to section to observe how life is preserved.

During midmorning, a call came over the loud-speaker. There is a lady patient who is returning for an emergency action. I almost fainted at the announcement. I presumed that it was Virgie, since she had just been operated on forty-eight hours earlier. Instead, it was a lady who was at the foot-end of Virgie's bed. This patient was a peasant person from South America. I found out all the details of who's who after the day was over.

Dr. Debakey was performing heart surgery on a very wealthy person from Boise, Idaho. This gentleman had been at the hospital for weeks building his strength to permit the surgery. Now in the middle of the process, the doctor leaves him and attends to the lady. The lady had a broken artery above the heart that had filled her chest cavity, and her life was affected. I recognized very quickly that Dr. DeBakey was not serving his clients because of wealth, but because of need. Since I was a clergyman, I was allowed to share my words with the recovering clients.

When I watched a man's surgery being delayed four hours to save another, I began to build a very strong feeling for the medical personnel who help save lives. From that day forward, I have been positively affected by the medical profession. Even now, when I am diagnosed for my personal needs, I ask the doctor for his diagnosis. Then I asked him for his prognosis. After the doctor's reports are concluded, I remind him that I have accepted all the medical reports and conclusions, but I will leave the final results in the hands of a wonderful God.

Great Fellowship

The next year at Ferndale was routinely normal. I was able to do everything that I had done when "the breakneck speed prevailed." Now I found time to be involved with the Michigan ministers in weekly fellowship activity. The close proximity of many churches to Detroit made it practical to enjoy sports' activities each week. We would assemble at the YMCA in midtown Detroit and play handball. The group was large enough that we had team-play for competition. Of all the different states where I had the privilege of working, the state of Michigan had the greatest fellowship among the ministers. This kind of friendship prevailed the eight years I lived in Michigan.

CHAPTER 15

EVANGELISM

"Do the work of an evangelist" (2 Timothy 4:5).

In the summer of 1969 during a state council session, a proposal was placed on the agenda that opened a new door. This terminology may seem trite. This was a new kind of venture in administrative work that had only begun in the general church and in other states where a third administrative position was financially feasible. It was proposed that Michigan follow the plan that other states were adopting. The position of state evangelism director was to be discussed.

State Evangelism Director

Brother Moore asked the council to decide who of that council might wish to accept this new position? All references were placed before us. The leading candidate was Carl (Jack) Allen. He was approved to be the new evangelism director. Now a slight deviation enters into the picture. The position has an appropriate base salary, but because of the minimal cash in our state budget, there are no funds for housing. Jack had just finished a large expansion of the Midland church, to which he had given his reserve money in that venture. The situation of his accepting this assignment without funds for housing brought him to resign the position after only one week.

I was second in line to be given the position. I accepted. The area of our administration was the state of

Michigan and the city of Windsor, Canada. During my first year in this new assignment, I had the unusual experience of being recognized by Wade H. Horton. He was the guest speaker at a conference in Windsor. Just three years earlier, he had given me a "political push" at Bailey Avenue, forcing my move from that church. Now he was congratulating me on my new position.

Big Brother–Little Brother Program

I had no guidelines to give me a sense of direction. The department was new to the general church. Consequently, I was at liberty to create my own program. The primary objective was to start new churches. To start a new mission, support must be arranged. The parent church would share a small group of members, along with financial support to sustain the new mission's survival.

It was a grand idea. To locate a place, share members, and give a continuing monetary support became a chore. Not every church was capable of doing what the proposal prescribed. I had to find some way to get started. My mind began a search for some kind of process to open the door of evangelism to start new churches. I fell upon the concept that I had read of a Catholic venture in orphanage support in Lincoln, Nebraska. A picture showed a small child being carried on the back of an adult. Their plan was identified as the "Big Brother Program."

The initial idea was taken as our foundation for opening new missions. The title for our plan was "Big Brother—Little Brother." The concept of adopting the plan was accomplished during the next state ministers business session. Even though not every church was strong enough to be a parent church, it was feasible that offerings could be given to support those places where new evangelism was reaching.

While the evangelism concept is very exciting, it was not very practical to attempt to get the job done in the dead of winter. I had just got started and then a different task was presented by Brother Moore. Estel had a bought a cottage on the Wimauma Campground in Tampa, Florida. He wanted me to go with him to build a garage for his personal needs. Since Evelyn had asked Virgie to go with her to Hawaii for a conference engagement, Estel felt that we could go to Florida and finish that small task while the ladies were enjoying an extended stay in Hawaii.

A Strange Event

The garage was built in one week. The midweek church service for campground residents was on Wednesday. I was asked to be the speaker for that service. A strange episode took place. At the conclusion of the service, I was asked to go to the church office to receive my offering. The clerk at Wimauma was none other than the Reverend Zeno C. Tharp. The same person who, as B. T. S. President had told me twenty-seven years earlier that I wasn't going to make it in school and the ministry, and I might as well go home. In his curt humor, he handed me a check for my sermon that evening and said, "Poor preach—poor pay."

Numerical Growth

The Michigan evangelism program was exciting. The state ministers rallied to the cause. As their new leader, I was invited to preach everywhere a door was open. The first year was primarily a seed-planting process. The support of the plan was accomplished by church pledges. The basic concept was for an adoption of a group of people by a mother church who would consider involvement to be their mission.

This plan was ultimately expanded to consider that a financially strong state would adopt a weaker, small state. This operation was adopted in our state. One of our prominent church leaders, Billy Bennett, pastor at the Steward Road Monroe church, was appointed by the Executive Committee to be the overseer of the state of Wisconsin. All the churches in Michigan adopted Wisconsin as their "Little Brother." The general purpose was dramatic. All of our church leaders in Michigan had very strong ties to Billy Bennett. He had ministered in Michigan for many years. He invited me to preach in their camp meeting and present this support concept.

This plan was also expressed often to other state leaders. It was exciting for me to learn that the general church, four years later when Ray Hughes was general overseer, was so interested in the concept that they adopted my plan across the nation to obtain the support of strong states to help weaker states. The process was not only to be financially helpful, but it would also send teams to their adopted state to evangelize an area, begin a new mission, and then continue to support that mission until it was strong enough to be organized as a self-supporting church.

Twenty-One New Churches

We had spread this good news all across the state. New missions were being organized. Because a new mission must have a facility in which to function, it was within my mandate to determine their ability to obtain an appropriate building. I had found that all too often a small operation collapses if it is overextended with its financial budget obligations. To be functional, a small mission must sustain a balanced budget. To buy a property under the assumption that they would grow into the numerical size to maintain a financial obligation was often the cause of that small mission's collapse and failure. During my five-year tenure as state evangelism director, I was responsible for organizing twenty-one churches under the supervision of three different state overseers. I served one year with Estel Moore, two years with Lewis J. Willis, and two years with Walter R. Pettitt.

All too soon the term of Estel Moore was ending. He finished his position in Michigan in 1970. The new term with Lewis Willis was a very pleasant and wonderful two years. While the state was making numerical growth, it was also establishing financial strength. The state offices had been in Pontiac for many years. I had remembered visiting C. R. Spain in Pontiac in 1956. Two new parsonages were approved while Brother Willis was state leader. One was for the overseer and one for the youth director. Those units were located in Royal Oaks and finished in due process. However, since funds were limited, there was not a capability to budget a new residence for my position. Because Brother Willis recognized the unusual predicament that was involved in my case, he permitted me to obtain my own home by either renting, buying, or permitting me to build my own home. I chose to build at 6809 Balmoral Terrace, Waterford. We moved into our new home in Waterford, located just a few miles northwest of Pontiac. My mortgage liability was not placed upon the state. For four years, I maintained my good status with my peers without being an extra financial obligation on the state budget.

During the decade of 1970, the mortgage market for church loans was very limited. The new rule of "hypothecate power" had only been ratified two years earlier at the General Assembly. It was difficult to find loan financing.

I researched and found a firm in Houston, Texas, that had a bond plan within their program. It was at this time that the Detroit Tabernacle was working on their program to move out of Detroit. They wanted to relocate in the Warren vicinity on 12 Mile Road, bordering the Detroit city limits. Paul Stallings, my former Missouri overseer, and now Tabernacle pastor sought my help. I was able to arrange the bond program and a new church was built by that plan.

In 1972-74, Walter R. Pettitt became state overseer. A strange quirk became a reference in my memory. In 1952 at the Indianapolis Coliseum, Walter Pettitt was standing in the hall waiting to get an interview with A. M. Phillips. I did not consider this little issue to be a problem to me this number of years later. Walter had two sisters who were members of the Ferndale church. I had learned who he was by his association with his family while I was pastor in Ferndale. We had two great years together.

It was near the end of my term. The four-year limitation rule of the general church would become my problem. Since the evangelism director's position in the organization was very new, there were no rules or policies whereby transfer to another state would allow a person to be assigned there. Contacts were made, but because the general church had not established interstate transfer polity, no other state position was available.

Ministry to the Military

Cecil Knight, assistant general overseer, had under his portfolio the jurisdiction of the Ministry to the Military. This also was a relatively new division of the church. Three months before the General Assembly, while visiting in our area, Cecil approached me about the possibility of me being assigned to the Far East, with all of the Hawaii military bases to be assigned to my portfolio and my office and residence to be Hawaii.

Five years earlier, Virgie and Evelyn Moore traveled to a conference in Hilo, Hawaii. When Virgie returned, she told me how she was captivated by the beauty of the Hawaiian Islands. Virgie also mentioned that for $5,000 she could have bought a lot in Hilo. At that time we didn't have but $1,000 in our savings account. So everything afterward about Hawaii was but a dream.

When Cecil told me about this new assignment, I got excited. I quickly told him that I would accept. The problem I faced was how do I sell my Waterford property on such short notice. After all, I had a mortgage that must be maintained and whatever profit I might have was conditioned on a sale.

Recalling God's Blessings

Does God guide through these complications? Yes! In summary, I advertised in the newspaper because I considered a realtor listing and closing might absorb all of my potential profit. One week before I was to leave Michigan, the property was leased with an option to buy at the end of twelve months. The option price was agreed upon. The new occupant was a qualified purchaser, and I received my profit of $5,000 one year later. That profit was my down-payment on my condo at 95-134 Kuahelani Avenue Apt. 118 in Mililani Town, Hawaii. Also, God blessed me with my pleasant Ferndale assignment. He also healed a sick wife. In addition, my Michigan evangelism position in new field church work was a great expansion in my ministry. Now He is opening a new door in one of the most exciting ministries of my life. That assignment was called "Far East—Ministry to the Military." Why will anyone question how God knows and directs?

CHAPTER 16

HAWAII

"Lift up your eyes on high, and behold. . . ."
(Isaiah 40:26).

In August of 1974, we arrived in the beautiful city of Honolulu, Hawaii. The greeting at the airport was "Aloha." This term means both hello and goodbye. It is used for a salutation of welcome or departure. Every person who left the airplane was presented with a lei of flowers of that wonderful island. Along with the flowers and the greeting was Hawaiian singing. If you didn't know anything about these Pacific Islands, you just might think you woke up in Paradise.

Virgie and I were excited from day one of our arrival. Since Virgie had been to Hawaii five years earlier at the Hilo Woman's Conference, she had a sensitivity of what we would find upon our arrival. We certainly were not disappointed. Our arrival schedule had been given to the church leaders in Honolulu. Not only did we sense the native mood of the greeting dancers but also the excitement of the church greetings.

Hawaii is the headquarters of the United States Pacific Command (USPACCOM), which comprises Army, Navy, Marine Corps and Air Force service components. The city of Aiea is the hub of this military area. It borders Honolulu to the west. Pearl Harbor Naval Base is a part of the Aiea city territory. The Hickam Air Force Base borders the Naval Base to the East. Fort Shafter Army Base is just east of Aiea in Honolulu. A Marine Base was on the opposite side of the island. Oahu is one of five major islands comprising the Hawaiian chain. The island's name of this metropolis is *Oahu*.

The YWEA project in Hawaii had just been completed the year before our arrival. The YWEA Center was located in Aiea.

My Hawaii Appointment

Does God guide through these complications? Yes! In summary, I advertised in the newspaper because I considered a realtor listing and closing might absorb all of my potential profit. One week before I was to leave Michigan, the property was leased with an option to buy at the end of twelve months. The option price was agreed upon. The new occupant was a qualified purchaser and I received my profit of $5,000 one year later. I rented my first year and bought my condo the second year.

The property I bought was in a new city that had been developed less than ten years earlier. The name of this area was called *Mililani Town*. It had been developed as a residential community. There were no industries or commercial projects in this community. It was ten miles from Aiea and four miles Schofield Barracks, Army Air Force Base in Wahiawa. The price was $55,250. Had we not had the funds available from the Michigan sale, we could not have prevailed in this action. I state this data to pinpoint a principle I grew up believing that I should never live on a plateau beyond my income. I further believe that to maintain a budget, one must maintain a lifestyle that stays within that income. If I had not been able to provide for my own residence when I was offered this assignment by the church, I do not believe the church would have given me the task of fulfilling the duties of this assignment. Why will anyone question how God knows and directs? My assignment was called "Far East—Ministry to the Military."

Beautiful Hawaii

My office was located in Aiea at 98-1022 Komo Mai Drive. The Youth World Evangelism Appeal (YWEA) project in Hawaii had just been completed the year before our arrival. The YWEA Center is located at 98-1022 Komo Mai Drive in Aiea. This beautiful building was designed to serve as a worship center for the military stationed nearby. Within this complex on the second floor was the Church of God Hawaii State Offices and the Far East Military office. This facility had been completed during the term of State Overseer Robert Fisher.

Bill Sheeks was appointed overseer of Hawaii the same year I was given the assignment of Far East Military Director. I had served my evangelism assignment in Michigan the same years that Sheeks was evangelism director in North Carolina. We did not arrive in Hawaii as strangers.

Since the overseer's house was a provision of the state assignment, the Sheeks family moved into their quarters upon arrival. I had to rent a house when I arrived. Our address for the first year was 98-1698 Nahele Street, Aiea, Hawaii.

Every day when I was in Hawaii, I would have connection to my office. For the first year of our Hawaii residency, we lived in a house less than three blocks from the center since a place to live was not provided in my salary structure. Twelve months later, the property transaction of our Waterford, Michigan, lease/purchase plan was finalized. I was able to receive the cash amount that permitted me to purchase property in Hawaii. We were now able to have our own house. The profit was my down payment on my condo at 95-134 Kuahelani Avenue, Apt. 118 in Mililani Town, Hawaii. I believe God was in the timing and the preservation of my profits.

I was appointed to a fairly new assignment with directions to live in Hawaii—a dream island. I had no parsonage in which to live, and my assignment had no written guidelines for me to follow or goals for me to reach. I had nothing but advice from several friends.

My Assignment

The Okinawa leader and my predecessor, Jesse L. Smith, was a sergeant while he was in the military. Jesse was the leader of the worship station that was located off-base. Smith had been a resident in Okinawa when he held the Far East position. I was told by Cecil Knight that the position of director had not reached the desired level of recognition under Smith's leadership. It was Knight's opinion that by my being in Hawaii and being interactive with the high level of the military, the assignment would be more achievable at every level of military authority. The advice of Cecil Knight to me was, "Get acquainted with the officer level."

How do I start? The task was not defined by any codebook. No military rules or guides were available. This job was virtually new to the Church of God. C. R. Spain held the military director position when he was at the executive level of the church. Knight became military director in 1972 as the official General Church representative.

When someone in the military asked for a worship center, then some kind of action would be taken. This was the situation in Japan. My brother, Ed, was a missionary in Japan from 1952 to 1965. While I do not have the exact history data of when he did a particular work, I saw a worship building near a military center in Misawa, Japan, with his name attached to the plaque on the wall of that center. This building was built sometime in the 1960 decade. Worship stations were also in Korea, Okinawa, Taipei, Philippines, and Guam. These centers were active under Church of God leadership.

How I Started

Since I was uncertain of how to get in touch with the military leaders, I began my work simply by attending the local church in Aiea. This was the building built by the YWEA program. The church was vibrant in their worship. Robert Fisher had appointed a minister for the church while he was the executive. The uniqueness of the Hawaii program was in a special new definition. Since all churches and pastors in the state were under the jurisdiction of the overseer, I was to serve in Hawaii, only as a representative for servicemen, on or off-base. When the same military were in Hawaiian churches, they were under the overseer's jurisdiction. Sheeks and I had worked together in the Evangelism Department. Now we were allies, but operating as leaders in a crossover activity.

When I got acquainted with military attendees to the center, I was invited by different ones to visit their base. While visiting those bases, I was able to identify with the base commanders. My direct contact on each base was with the chaplain who served on that base.

Pearl Harbor

I made contact with the Naval Base at Pearl Harbor. The chaplain at Pearl Harbor was very friendly. When I defined the magnitude of my assignment, I was informed that because of continued military involvement in Vietnam, I would not be able to travel to one of the places Cecil Knight had directed me to reach.

The chaplain informed me, however, that he was the command chaplain of the Pacific. He said, "I can help you get to any base in the Pacific if you will work under my supervision." My answer was a very quick yes.

I had sent notice to the different leaders of the centers that were under our church jurisdiction that I was the new appointee for servicemen to the Far East. I had set schedules and confirmed my air travel dates for my travel circuit to all centers where I would be ministering. I was waiting for the military approval for my Thailand clearance.

From the time I left the chaplain's office until my orders were issued was about six weeks. Before I heard from the Pearl Harbor chaplain, I was contacted by Chaplain Hugo Hammond (CPT) USNR by phone from Okinawa. This is the first time I remember a phone call from anywhere outside the U.S.A. Since Hugo was married to a girl I knew from the Texas days on the campground, we knew each other. One of the first words he said was, "What in the world did you do to get the rank of *general*?"

In shock, I replied, "I do not know what you are talking about; what do I do?"

He said, "The first thing you do is keep your shoes shined and your hair combed. The next step is to keep your suit pressed when you go to the Base Commander's office to present your credentials when you arrive on his base." Hugo had received the military information at the time my position was granted from Washington. I had not yet been informed by the Pearl Harbor chaplain.

When Pearl Harbor Naval Office called to notify me of my clearance, I was overwhelmed. I had been granted Civil Service Rank of GS–16–E. This was interpreted by the chaplain as being equivalent to one star (Brigadier General). Military communication gave my status and authority to all base commanders in the Far East.

When the Pearl Harbor chaplain handed me 24 sets of orders, I had an additional shock. My name had been misspelled. Wayne HELL was not the way I wished to say who I was. When I pointed out the error of my misspelled name, and the fact that my travel schedule had already been confirmed, the chaplain said, "Just make apology to each command officer for the wrong spelling. It will take another six weeks to get corrected spelling on your orders." Because of his comment, I remembered his previous statement: "I can help you if you will work under my supervision." I followed his directive.

It was a dramatic experience. Each base commander was extremely cordial. At each time of my arrival to a base, I was provided an escort. The escort would be a person of rank. His rank would be from lieutenant to lieutenant colonel.

I was further informed by my Pearl Harbor chaplain that no chaplain who is commissioned will ever have a rank above colonel unless he is stationed in Washington, D. C. This had dramatic meaning. I would always be granted the ultimate courtesy, recognition, and respect wherever I would travel in this assignment.

I made my schedule to each country of my jurisdiction, setting the times to allow me to get acquainted with the leaders of each center. It was a very enlightening experience to visit countries of Asia for the first time. I had heard much about Japan since Ed and Letha had served as missionaries in Yokahama for fifteen years. They gave me a picture of a Japanese couple when they were on furlough in 1956. I cherish that picture even today.

South Korea

I arrived in Seoul, Korea, during winter. Reverend Ron Byrne was the director of the fellowship at Yongsan. This is a suburb of Seoul, the capital of South Korea. One of the unusual incidents was to walk into the house and feel the heat of the floor. The system of heating the house was in the floor. When one entered a room, the shoes were removed. There was no furnace to blow heat. Everybody wore extra heavy clothing to stay warm. It was difficult for me to adapt to this cold weather because I did not bring enough clothes to adjust to the cold temperature.

The fact that the military bases of South Korea were prominent was conditioned by the North Korea/South Korea conflict being unsettled. When I first arrived in 1974, the United States forces in South Korea were dominant all over that country.

The largest U. S. base was in Yongsan. As a suburb of Seoul, it was easy to have access to the capital. My visits to the gift shops were made possible by the Church of God Overseer, Yung Chul Han. Brother Han and I became great friends. He had been in the Church of God for many years. Now, I was able to lean on him as well as the connections I had with the military to visit any military base I desired. The Yong San military facility was a key location for developing a military center in Korea.

Okinawa

From South Korea, I made my next stop in Okinawa. This is one of the famous locations where many battles were fought during World War II. The Okinawa Center for the military was just a short distance from the Kadena Air Force Base. Here I met the director of the Okinawa Center. Charles Wright was pastor of this center. It was located in Oyama, just a couple of miles from Kadena AFB. The Okinawa Center was considered the most central of the five locations I supervised within the church organization. It became the most used facility for easy military access, whether north from Korea, south from the Philippines, or west from Guam. The retreats that convened in Hawaii were always considered local to Hawaii and no travel from Asia was attached to the Hawaii retreats.

Taiwan

Leaving Okinawa and flying south, my next stop was Taiwan. SFC John Reeves was the person in charge at this military station. My mail was dispatched six weeks before I was to arrive in Taiwan. The military facility was a great distance from Taipei. When my plane landed at the Taipei Airport, no one was there to greet me. I was to check into the hotel and await my escort to the base. When I waited and waited, I decided to walk around the block where I was to spend the night. After two hours, I checked into a room and began my attempt to phone Sergeant Reeves. Unfortunately, the telephone operator was Chinese and did not understand my language. Over and over I thought, *if I keep trying, I will find a telephone operator who will understand English*. After six hours of futile efforts, I finally reached a phone operator who was bilingual. When I reached Sergeant Reeves, he said, "I was unable to come because I was sick." To say the least, I was able to sleep that night and leave for my next destination in spite of this failure to connect in person.

Hong Kong

Flying into Hong Kong was a beautiful experience. Hong Kong is an independent city from the country of China. My contact there was not military-related. Lovell and Ginny Cary had moved to this great city and were headquartered there to make it central to all their connections in the World Mission position Lovell had at this time. Having been a missionary to Haiti, and knowing that the Carys had been missionaries to Hawaii before it became a state, I knew Lovell and Ginny for two decades. Now to be a guest in their home in Hong Kong and reminisce on their work in the Orient was a great delight.

I needed to know the contacts in missions in the Philippines so that I would be able to intermingle these connections with my military ones. I spent a number of days with Lovell and Ginny. During this time, Lovell arranged for me to go to the border of mainland China for a view of that great land. Since I had no connection to allow me to enter China, I contented myself with the event of looking and leaving. I met friends of the Carys when we went out for a splendid Chinese dinner at a very high-class restaurant. One thing I learned was that the entrées are all placed in the center of the table. You take from that bowl by using your fingers. The end result is that you will leave a trail of drippings or food between the center of the table to your plate. The classification to this situation by the chef and, or the server is, "The more mess you have made, the better you enjoyed it."

Philippines

Entering Manila Airport is similar to any other commercial location. The airport is filled with passengers going and coming. My greeters were the missionaries Lovell had notified of my arrival. The Philippine society is very friendly. Having been the geographical territory of much activity during World War II, it is an international hub for travelers everywhere in Asia. Since I wished to spend time with the strong mission work of the Philippines, I scheduled to go to Clark Air Force Base with my mission friends as my escorts.

Clark Air Force Base in the Philippines is located about fifty miles from Manila at Angeles City. The Pentecostal Servicemen's Center is located just off-base. The center was directed by James Hancock. As each center was always just a few miles from a major base, it was convenient for me to access any personnel on base or off base at any time. The reason for this option was that I had the equivalent rank of Brigadier General and could come in or out of any base after I had submitted my credentials. This base became a place of frequent visits during my tenure in the Far East.

I was able to arrange expansion of the Philippine Servicemen's Center chapel in a unique way. Because Philippine missions were so strong with the native population, it was concluded that we needed to get their local support in worship services along with the military. Philippine law determined that eventually the Clark Air Force base would soon be released from United States authority to Philippine control. I made contact with the World Missions Department and helped arrange for the title of this center to be re-titled to the Missions Department. From this posture, and with funds from World Missions, we were able to build a large new chapel under the direction of Director Darrel Rose.

During my second trip to the Philippines, while I was spending a month to assist in the building of the new retreat chapel, I had a strange experience. Chaplain John Ward (Cpt) USAF had been transferred from Thailand to Clark Air Force base. This event had stunning reaction throughout the military facility at Clark.

One evening a military plane embarked on a trip to the U.S.A. Chaplain Ward was a passenger on the flight. After about two hours in flight, it was rumored that a bomb was onboard the aircraft. According to the reports recorded thereafter, a serious event happened. Chaplain Ward concluded that since he was the senior officer on the plane in his military classification, he would exercise his authority to demand the pilot of this aircraft to return to Clark. His premise was "to secure the lives of the passengers before the bomb exploded and killed all on board." At midnight upon arrival at Clark, the commanding general of the base was duly called to the aircraft, and the plane was evacuated and inspected for the potential bomb. The results were negative. But the following morning, the Clark Air Force Base was buzzing with the event of the aircraft's midnight return.

During the next week, the chaplains of the base were furious about Chaplain Ward and his purported policy.

The gossip about the ethics of this same chaplain made everyone on base who knew of this event quite reactionary. Chaplain Ward did not survive long in his tenure at Clark. The next thing I knew, Ward was transferred back to the mainland.

Guam

My visit to Guam was extraordinary. The Yigo Pentecostal Serviceman's Center was directed by Lester Spencer. This location was just a short distance from Anderson Air Force Base. At this base, Major General, Charles F. Minter accepted me with my credentials and my misspelled name. His acknowledging of the name *HELL* brought a speedy reaction in his acceptance greeting. He said, "I'm glad your first name isn't *Raisin* or you wouldn't be welcome on my base." Major General Minter was an attendant at one of our future retreats. (This event was covered in chapter 1.)

At Agana Naval Base I was extended the privilege of entering a U. S. Submarine powered by a nuclear reactor engine. This was a high experience for me.

Oh! My Sunburn

The local center at Yigo had two FAA technicians who attended services regularly. At Guam I experienced an event that gave me serious consequences. Tom Antles and Van Laurents, two FAA technicians, along with Director Charles Wright and I went out on a catamaran to snorkel. At early morning, the low tide caused the ocean water to be too shallow for all four of us to get away from shore because of the extensive coral growth. Subsequently, Tom took Charles Wright and me two miles from shore to see the marine life at the edge of the shallow shelf, just before it goes miles deep. Tom then went back to pick up Van and returned to where we had been let out of the catamaran.

Two miles from shore, two of us put on our snorkeling gear. Because I was not a good swimmer, I had taken a rubber tire tube and tied myself to it. When I exited the catamaran, I stood upon a huge coral rock about four feet in diameter on the ocean floor. Panic seized me because I was rising and falling with the ebb of the tide. I thought about my foolishness to be two miles from shore and just one friend to help me. After ten minutes of hyperventilating, I settled down and began to breathe normally. I began my viewing of the marine life. The four of us would make this day a classic event.

I had borrowed a sport shirt and a pair of pants from one of the local guys in Guam. What happened during those next hours of my swimming experience became my next real problem. When I got back to the center, I found I had a three-inch wide purple burn to my back. This purple colored skin ultimately became a melanoma skin cancer. Two years later I received a doctor's notice about the severity of my Guam adventure. Removing that cancer became the first of seven cancer episodes of my lifetime.

Thailand

Traveling to Thailand was a fulfillment of my military assignment. Cecil Knight had given me a strong directive to look into and resolve a serious situation with an U Dorn chaplain. I had my first contact in Bangkok, Thailand, with the dean of Church of God chaplains. Edward E Shoupe (LTC) USAF was stationed in Bangkok. Before we went to U-Dorn Air Base, Chaplain Shoupe escorted me to an air base on the coast of Thailand. We walked along the runway and watched planes take off. On one event, Chaplain Shoupe said to me, "You didn't see that." I noticed a plane leave the runway and within seconds, it was out of sight. It was totally black in color. It was one of the Air Force phantom jets, a plane that was used all over the world in secret missions for the U.S.

Washington D.C. had authorized me as a GS–16–E, and Chaplain Shoupe, my escort, was a Lieutenant Colonel. We were sent to U-Dorn in a military aircraft. Upon arrival, we were greeted by the base commander. The base chaplain, having been informed by Sergeant Snavely of our pending arrival, was very snobbish to his commander. When informed that a general and a colonel and eighteen enlisted men were arriving, the chaplain said to his commander, "He ain't no general; he's a preacher."

SSgt. R. L. Snavely was the chaplain's assistant. The reason Sergeant Snavely wanted help was knowledge I had received earlier. I had known Bob Snavely since my days in Michigan. He was a young credentialed minister from the Big Rapids District. His base (Chaplain John Ward (Cpt) USAF) was credentialed with the Pentecostal Church of God of North America. Ward's theology principles were being advocated in his military church services. The issue in question was in his attempt to teach worshipers how to "speak in tongues." This was not any part of Snavely's theology principles. Snavely was unwilling to subscribe to that practice. Yet, to be negative to his command superior, made him subject to military discipline. We resolved the issue with dignity. Snavely was not in jeopardy. Chaplain Wood was reassigned.

CHAPTER 17

MILITARY MISSION

"The Lord hath done great things for us"
(Psalm 126:3).

Because Hawaii suffered dramatically from the Japanese actions that triggered World War II, the military has strengthened their positions accordingly. The economy of Hawaii is conditioned by the strength of the military budget. I committed my time and energy to becoming adept in a military way in every phase of my work. Not having served in the military before this assignment, I was intrigued by the principles and procedure that servicemen followed for their normal and regular routine. I realized that I would need to adapt to each regimen to accomplish my tasks. Along with these schedules, I found a very pleasant and exciting time of friendship, fellowship, and pleasure in living this new lifestyle.

My Hawaiian Ministry

Hawaii is located over 2,000 miles from the west coast of North America. Church mission emphasis brought much church growth to these islands, and they were filled with native Hawaiians. It was a delight to minister to these people. They had customs very different from those in the continental congregations.

My interaction with these groups became a splendid policy to develop treasured friendship and fellowship. I ministered to churches throughout the islands.

Retreat Time

When it came time to set the schedule for what we called *Military Retreats*, we met with military and native attendants. We also worked with the state office, since local churches would also be invited to participate in the military retreats. This way, both the native and military attendants would be blessed.

The Hawaii Military Retreats had been established a few years before I came to the state. My first retreat at the Aiea Center convened in the spring of 1975. In March 1976, the advertising defined it to be the 8th annual retreat in Hawaii. The director in charge in 1975 was Ron Smith. He was replaced with Richard Shelton. Both of these men did great work with the military.

During the 1976 retreat, Billy Rayburn, overseer from Alaska, was the night speaker. We had over 500 present for the three-night affair. The center had been dedicated two years earlier, July 21, 1974, and now it seemed as though there had been no better place chosen to have retreats.

The year of 1976 was a very special year. I was able to travel during my two-year term from 1974 to 1976 with a lot of activity on every front. After getting my military clearance, I stayed busy. All those details were expressed in the previous chapter. I now settled down to the routine. While I was in my home venues, I kept busy with visits to all bases and chaplains. I made special friends with those who attended the retreat center weekly. It was a pleasure to have many of them invite me to play golf. I was permitted to play by paying the military fee of $6 per game. I played three times a week when I was not on foreign travel.

A Very Special Year–1976–but All Was Not Well

I spent six weeks in Okinawa during June and July 1976. Our director, Charles Wright, decided to return to the United States for the General Assembly and then enlist in school. As a military person, he had filled the position at Okinawa with great dignity. What made this date special was that it was the 200-year-old anniversary of the U.S.A. The military celebrated this event with fireworks all day long. That night the sky was aglow with all the fireworks. I returned to my Hawaii home and the joy of being with Virgie.

During this summer of 1976, I heard Virgie express her moods about her failing health. When we made our jaunt to McDonalds each week, she continued to question things about her life.

As I have stated in chapter 1 of this writing, everything seemed to be in a whirl. I had my vision and the "BUT GOD" evidence of that month and the following five months were beyond my logic to understand.

38th Parallel–Korea

When Virgie and I went to Alaska for their first retreat, we parted our traveling ways to go in opposite directions. Virgie went to Dallas and I went to Korea. Our Korea retreat was the last week of October, 1976. I was escorted to the DMZ and had the unusual episode of eating at the table where the building sits on the line that defines the boundaries of North and South Korea. On one side of the table were the South Koreans and on the opposite side sat the North Koreans. There was a very tense mood among the people in that room.

It was two months earlier that the "hatchet incident" occurred. On August 18, 1976, in the Joint Security Area (JSA) territory between the two nations which provided a neutral zone between North and South Korea, an event took place that almost brought the United States back into a war with North Korea. Since I do not remember all the details of my visit to the DMZ, I will cite the Wikipedia Encyclopedia for the specific particulars.

In the JSA near the Bridge of No Return, a 100-foot poplar tree blocked the line of sight between a United Nations Command (UNC) checkpoint (CP#3) and observation post (OP#5).

CP#3 situated next to the Bridge of No Return, was the northernmost UNC checkpoint and only visible from OP#5 during the winter months. During the summer months, only the top of CP#3 was visible from one other UNC checkpoint (CP#2). Running across the middle of the bridge was the Military Demarcation Line between North Korea and South Korean territories.

The proximity to North Korean territory and the North Korean checkpoints on all access routes, along with the repeated attempts to kidnap the UNC personnel working there, led to CP#3 being referred to as "The Loneliest Outpost in the World."

On one occasion before the incident, North Korean soldiers held a group of U.S. troops at gunpoint, so Joint Security Force (JSF) Company Commander Captain Arthur Bonifas was sent to force the North Koreans to stand down and bring the Americans back to safety, which he did successfully. Bonifas was one of the two killed in the axe murder.

The Incident–Axe Murder

On August 18, 1976, a group of five Korea Service Corps (KSC) personnel escorted by a UNC security team consisting of Bonifas, his South Korean (ROK)Army counterpart, Captain Kim, the platoon leader in the area (1LT Mark Barrett) and eleven enlisted personnel, both American and South Korean, went into the JSA to trim the tree as previously scheduled with the KPA delegation. The two captains did not wear side arms, as members of the Joint Security Area were limited to only five armed officers and thirty armed enlisted personnel at a time. However, there were mattocks in the back of the 2½-ton truck. The KSC workers had the axes they brought to prune the tree branches. The tree had been scheduled to be trimmed seven days earlier, but rain had forced the work to be rescheduled.

After trimming began, fifteen to sixteen North Korean soldiers appeared, commanded by Senior Lieutenant Pak Chul, whom the UNC soldiers had previously nicknamed "Lieutenant Bulldog" due to a history of confrontations. Pak and his subordinates appeared to observe the trimming without concern for approximately 15 minutes until he abruptly told UNC to cease activity, stating the tree could not be trimmed "because Kim Il Sung personally planted it and nourished it and it's growing under his supervision." Captain Bonifas ordered the detail to continue, and turned his back on Lieutenant Pak Chul.

After being ignored by Captain Bonifas, Pak sent a runner across the Bridge of No Return. Within minutes a North Korean guard truck crossed the bridge and approximately 20 more North Korean guards disembarked carrying crowbars and clubs. Pak again demanded that the tree-trimming stop, and when Captain Boniface again turned his back on him, Pak swung a karate chop to the back of Captain Boniface's neck. Captain Boniface died instantly. Lieutenant Barrett died en route to the hospital in Seoul.

Anticlimax

The "Axe Murder" event happened just over two months before my fall retreat at Yongsan. I had made my schedule to visit the various bases that were on my outpost area of contact. I had heard of the "Axe Murder" event and decided to visit the DMZ. This visit was made after our retreat schedule was over.

When I finished the visit to the North Korean border and observed the area where the "Agreement" to settle the conflict between North and South Korea was signed, I felt as though I was at the peace table during the truce days of the early 1950 decade when North and South Korea called the 38th parallel their dividing line.

When that episode of my story was complete, I went back to Seoul and was given the opportunity to visit with the base commander. I was given a very broad reference to the extreme conditions that prevailed during the event described above. I was informed that I was the first civilian to whom this event had been shared since the Axe Murders happened—the event that brought the United States within minutes of returning to war against North Korea.

News About Virgie

The day was hardly over when I was given a report from my military associates, by way of military radio, about Virgie. The message was brief but gave specific information about her being in a hospital in Dallas. The phone numbers were available. However, because there is a 14-hour difference between these two cities, I had to wait until midnight to make my contact to Dallas. My first words to Virgie were the quotation of Psalm 73:26: "My flesh and my heart faileth, but God (my emphasis) is the strength of my heart and my portion forever."

As explained in the first chapter of this writing, everything about the episodes, which became the main event and focal point, was coming to a climax. I declare that in all the complexities of my life, my story continues. But God was and is a part of every minute of the events that created this story. I left South Korea just as soon as the military people could arrange my departure. Because of the issues of travel, I had to return first to Hawaii and then to Dallas. (Read again chapter 1 to find out all the details of the solutions obtained.)

After Dallas

When everything about Virgie's surgery was over and she was dismissed, we headed back to our lovely home in Mililani Town. In the next couple of months, we enjoyed the time and conditions that seemed to make us feel that things were getting back to normal.

Frank and Kohatha Culpepper visited us just after Christmas. Dr. Culpepper had been elected to the Executive Committee the previous August. His portfolio now made him my boss. I had known the Culpepper family only since the time I was considered in 1964 to possibly be the overseer of Oregon. The Culpepper appointment as overseer of Oregon preempted my appointment there.

I had an extraordinary relationship with the Culpepper family since 1964. I shared with Brother Culpepper about the conditions of my extensive travel time away from Virgie. I knew my schedule had an unwritten requirement that I would be on my Pacific circuit every four months. I would be away from home from four to six weeks at a time. I had considered the problem I was to deal with about extended travel and my need to help Virgie. Expressing these issues with my new boss, I felt that I might be in jeopardy if I did not do everything "by the book" according to his style of leadership.

My Resignation

When I finished my remarks about my travel conditions, I posed a calculated question, asking that I be allowed to surrender my position at the General Assembly in 1978. I felt that I needed to be available for Virgie in case of need, and I did not wish to be otherwise inefficient in my duties. I did not expect an answer about the request. Time would tell how things would go.

When I returned to my local activities in Hawaii in 1977, life was at its peak. Virgie was doing very well and I was maintaining my normal rapport with everybody local and by mail with my leaders in the Pacific. Because of the need to help Virgie in performing her normal routine, I spent more time at home.

Back to the Books

During this period, I spent s lot of study time in my education requirements to obtain my B.A. degree from

Lee. I had been an eager learner of required classes when I started my studies. I happened to be a dropout when I finished the eighth grade. When I entered B.T.S. it was to find a status in ministry. When I graduated in 1944, I concluded I was ready and willing to apply my training to do what God had called me to do. When I came back to Lee in 1947, I came as a third-year Christian Education student. When the dean at Lee, Dr. E. C. Tapley, granted me college credits for my studies if I made the grade requirement, I became a college student. I went to Universities in Houston, St. Louis, and Detroit with the idea that I could learn something. I did not attempt to finish a program that would grant me a degree.

Now, thirty years later, I decided to finish my work in what Lee had provided to people like me in the Extension Department. I was required to take 30 hours of study by extension to receive my degree. After thirty years on my record and 188 hours on my transcript, in May 1977, Virgie and I scheduled a flight from Honolulu to Atlanta. We drove to Cleveland and I was welcomed to become the first student to graduate from the Lee Extension Department. I was greeted by Lee College authorities as a graduating alumnus. I received my degree and made my preparation to go back home.

Unexpected Transition Time

My intent to fulfill protocol requirements had me contacting the General Offices the day after I graduated. Cecil Knight was the general overseer. When I made my appointment that morning, I went to the Executive Board meeting for the first time since I had been given my assignment as director of the Pacific—Far East Ministry to the Military. I had consented to this position three months prior to the 1974 General Assembly. In 1976, I was reassigned for my second term. I was now asking them for a short time to share my greetings since I was in town. I had not had any contact with any general church board or executive-level group since I had been appointed in 1953 to Haiti.

I had a very pleasant time with the committee. I was invited out to lunch with Floyd Timmerman and Frank Culpepper. We talked and laughed about good ole' days. Midway in our lunch schedule, a remark was made about comments I had made to Frank Culpepper in January about reassignment at the next General Assembly. I was shocked. I did not want to ask for relief now. After lunch, Virgie and I went to Chattanooga to shop. About 3 p.m. I received a call asking me to come to the headquarters' office. I hedged about going. The secretary said, "If I were you . . . you'd better come right now."

I walked in and saw the committee around the table. Each one was somber and expressing himself in due process. I heard reports that made me feel jumpy inside. I heard good reports that made me happy. Suddenly, General Overseer Knight spoke. "We wanted to be more specific this morning, but circumstances had not yet been worked out. We have a very big announcement to make. As of now, you are no longer representative to the military in the Pacific Far East. As of this minute, you have been appointed as overseer of the state of New Jersey."

I nearly collapsed in shock. Cecil Knight informed me that Wayne Taylor, the overseer had resigned, but the committee had not been able to finalize his reassignment earlier that morning. By noon, things had been settled and

Taylor was going back to Alabama. Taylor's reasons were serious because of a racial problem. The Taylor family had teenage children and the school district where the children were placed was in an all-Negro district. The children had finished their nine-month school year. However, the parents were perplexed over the fact that they would have to spend the next three years in a dominant Black culture. This was the cause of Brother Taylor's request to be released. When the church was assigned for him to return to Loxley, Alabama, everything fell in place on that same day for my new appointment.

CHAPTER 18

STATE OVERSEER ASSIGNMENT

*"Be instant in season, out of season:
reprove, rebuke, exhort...."*
(2 Timothy 4:2).

When I was appointed to be overseer of New Jersey, I was in a state of excitement as well as instant shock. The details of this event were spelled out at the end of chapter 17.

I had always esteemed the level of leadership as an overseer to be the ultimate of my life's work. When I was finishing my work as the missionary leader of Haiti in 1956, I was asked by one of the executive leaders if I would be willing to accept the assignment as overseer to Montana at the next General Assembly. Being a very young person at that time and only having completed fourteen years in my schooling and new church work, I felt that I needed to be a good pastor before I should be able to tell a subordinate person how to do his task. Therefore, I declined the option of serving as overseer at that time.

When I had fulfilled eight years of pastoral duties in my position in St. Louis, I was again asked if I would be willing to serve as overseer of Oregon. I consented, but was bypassed in 1964. Frank Culpepper was appointed and I went to pastor in Mississippi. Now, thirteen years later, and after two wonderful assignments—State Evangelism Director of Michigan and Military Representative to the Far East in Hawaii and the Orient—I have been chosen. I was taking over the balance of the two-year term of Wayne Taylor. I would have thirteen months of his term to establish my status. I could not foreknow what would happen, **But God** foreknew.

Transition

I was asked by the Executive Committee to hasten back to Hawaii, close out my office, and leave all of my unfinished tasks in the military operations to Bill Sheeks. I was to be in my new location in ten days. This meant packing and arranging for air freight of my belongings.

My biggest problem was my real estate. My mortgage was ongoing. I would have to put my property up for sale. The speed in doing this was too big for me to fathom. The option I had to take was to attempt a sale conditioned by a lease/rental.

In the course of time, it became evident that real estate sales were nil. I had the realtor place a renter in the condo. There were plenty of military people who would rent because their term in the military was always limited. The difficulty I faced at the time of my transfer was that my mortgage note was $450 per month and my rental income was only $350 per month. This condition was absolute. I fast forward in this paragraph to pinpoint a variable that would occur in the next decade. Economy and inflation factors brought rent up from $350 per month to $1,000 per month. Whereas I could not sell when I left Hawaii, I was able to maintain full occupancy in renters and double my mortgage payments because of increased rental income. I paid off the loan of my mortgage in fifteen years rather than the original thirty-year plan.

My Work as Overseer Begins

I moved into the state office home. My new address was 4 Longview Avenue, Freehold, New Jersey 07728. This city was a beautiful area of the eastern United States. Freehold was just 45 miles south of New York City. It was also a thriving area of the state for horse racing. Colts Neck, a neighboring town, was an area where horses were bred. Because of the type of land needed to be used for horseracing, this area was teeming with farms where these racehorses were bred and kept. There was a stadium in Freehold and horseracing was a standard activity.

One of the conditions that seemed to have great prominence was that New Jersey was on overflow area to New York City. When migrant people wished to become permanent residents, it was most often that New York City was the primary entrance to the U.S. It became a standard phrase to say that this area was the melting pot of foreign immigrants.

The township of Freehold had a population of around 25,000 and was primarily a melting pot, overflow territory, and residency area for all classes of immigrants. The section of the town where we lived had mostly Black residents. This was the reason for Wayne Taylor's resignation. His family would be compelled to be in the Black community school system for his entire term in New Jersey.

The Black Culture

What makes this part of my story interesting is related to Black culture. While serving as missionary in Haiti beginning in 1953, I was able to work and travel to all the countries of the Caribbean. I had no difficulties in working with anyone in Black-culture countries. Having been born in the north of the United States, I was not influenced by the inter-warp culture that prevailed in the South.

Now twenty-four years later, I am the spiritual leader of twenty-nine churches in New Jersey. The majority of these churches were Black congregations. This did not cause me any problems. What was unusual was that in spite of the issue that the congregation was Black, each church group worshiped according to its culture and sometimes its language. The Haitians were just like the people I knew in Haiti. Since migrating to the U.S., they had learned the English language, but they still worshiped as Haitians worship.

The Jamaican migrants worshiped Jamaican-style. The Bahamians worshiped Bahamas-style. I had a Yugoslavian congregation that worshiped according to their European culture. Last but not least were the northeastern white culture class of people whose worship was different from the other groups.

What was exciting to me was that I felt that I had been preschooled in how to adapt to this complex cultural group of churches in what I called the overflow of the melting pot of people. Since no one group of Black congregations of different country nationality held a majority among this group of twenty-nine churches, it was not difficult for them to accept a white leader.

A pleasant experience occurred when I visited New York City. The overseer, J.D. Golden, had worked in the metropolitan area of Chicago in his earlier ministry. We had known each other since our days of interaction when we pastored churches in Missouri and Illinois. The biggest church in metro Brooklyn was a Haitian church. The pastor of this church was an electrician in Haiti who helped me build the Haiti Compound twenty-plus years earlier. He was now the leading Haitian minister in the U.S.A. We had great services together whenever camp meeting time came for each state.

In summary, the northern section of New Jersey contained about four of our white churches. The mid-central section of New Jersey contained the Black congregations, and the southern section of the state had all white churches.

I lived only fifteen miles from Princeton University. It was always nice to have visitors to come our way who were students at Princeton doing graduate work.

Adapting and Adjusting

I was able to adapt to the leaders of all of our Black churches without any difficulty. It was a pleasant experience. I had similar experiences with all of our white leaders. Everything worked so well that we were able to outgrow numerically and financially (our mission-state status) within our general church organization rank in the balance of the fifteen months (General Assembly term) left from the Wayne Taylor term. When I was reappointed for the next term in 1978, I encountered a financial problem. Since the state had grown to a non-mission state status, our office could no longer receive funds from the national office. We were now considered a self-supporting state. This made it very difficult to sustain our financial obligations as we had in the past. We were pressed to develop a financial plan within the state to ask for finances to help us. We created a theme and preached about this plan. The title of our theme was "ENJOY" (**E**vangelize **N**ew **J**ersey **O**ffer **Y**ourself). This program was implemented with a chorus I created and sang in our church services.

Complications

After one year of exceptional spiritual growth among the churches, I settled down to the routine of visiting churches, encouraging ministers, and socializing with all classes of all nationalities.

We developed a good bond with all of our leaders and churches. During the middle of my second term as overseer, I received a shocking phone call, informing me that the pastor of one of our churches was not living according to Christian principles mandated by the Bible and dictated by the Church of God. The caller explained the situation fully.

Because the magnitude of this allegation involved a prominent minister, I called General Overseer Ray Hughes, who gave me specific instructions of how to pursue the next course of action. According to church policy, I was responsible for total control of the allegations until it could be determined if this church leader must face these issues in a church trial. For me, It was a war of nerves. This incident happened in midsummer of 1979. I had to live through the routine of all events we faced when state council sessions were held. This accused minister was a leading member of the state council.

When it was finally determined that this minister must stand trial, I was in a state of apprehension. What happens if every issue purported to be fact is not conclusively proven? I was shocked when the minister said to me, "You better be sure of what you are going to do. You will either destroy me or I will destroy you."

The State Trial Board convened the last week of October 1979. Because of validity of the evidence submitted, a verdict of guilty was charged, and a revocation of the minister's ordination credentials was rendered by that state board.

Church function is dependent upon leadership. Leaders are selected by the rules and policies that mandate a strict adherence to Biblical standards. Also, inherent with these criteria are the conditions that day-to-day operations must comply with the principles of church polity and policy. If there is a violation to church procedure, there must be action to correct it. If it involves the violator, similar action must be taken or the system breaks down. The follow-up to this situation mandated that this minister be released from his leadership role as pastor of the local church.

When I went to the local church the next Sunday to take action to install a new pastor, I was informed that the church had seceded from the Church of God organization. This was a new problem. Legally, religious church policy as defined by organization rule of law, was violated. I was now faced with a much larger, complicated, civil lawsuit to define and defend our church law.

The next day I called the general overseer, who gave specific instructions of what I must do in order to maintain the authority of Church of God policy as determined by the polity of our organization. Brother Hughes informed me that I must be on the platform every time a scheduled service convened.

It would be this episode that would indicate that my authority within my state overseer portfolio was not being abdicated. For the next two and one half months, I was prohibited to speak at the church service for any purpose.

As a result, I sat on the platform every Sunday, morning and night, and Wednesday night.

The lawsuit was filed in the Superior Court of New Jersey, Chancery Division, Cumberland County. The attorney firm of Greenblatt & Greenblatt filed a duly Verified Complaint in the matter. CHURCH OF GOD, etc, et al, Plaintiffs, vs. CALVARY CATHEDERAL, et al, Defendants were listed in a Civil Action—ORDER TO SHOW CAUSE. What became so unusual to me was this transaction was filed on November 15, 1979, my 55th birthday.

An ORDER OF INTERLOCUTORY INJUNCTION ACTION was entered on January 11, 1980, and was made permanent on February 13, 1980. A further Civil Action ORDER on June 27, 1980, permanently enjoined and restrained the DEFENDANTS—CALVARY CATHEDRAL et al.

When the courts indicated that the Calvary Cathedral must give back to the Church of God their property, which was being attempted to be gained by secession, I then had the platform and the pulpit under my jurisdiction. That was a daily part of my routine for eight and one-half months following the church trial and then by the civil trial. I had only fifteen days after the civil court verdict until the Church of God convened the next General Assembly. I would then be appointed to another state.

CHAPTER 19

LOOKING BACK

"But my God shall supply all your need according to his riches in glory by Christ Jesus"
(Philippians 4:19).

As a young boy, I was taught by my parents to be frugal. I came from a family of ten children. I was the oldest, born in 1924. My next sibling was named Deryl, born in 1925. He took the nickname "Tex" as a teenager. The next sibling was L.E. (Ed) born in 1927. Next came Darvel, born in 1928. A.C. (Punk) was born in 1929. Five years would pass and we would go through the beginning of the great depression of the 1930 decade. In 1934, J.H.(Gebo) became the sixth sibling of our family. Next was the only girl. In 1935, Wanda was born; in 1937, Dean became number eight; in 1939 David was born, and in 1941, just before World War II, Mom had her last child. His name was Daniel. We all called him Dan.

The Depression Years

Henry and Thelma Heil fought the trauma of the Depression years to work at keeping twelve mouths fed and everyone clothed. We had hand-me-down clothes on an ongoing basis until Wanda. Then mom began to sew pretty clothes for her and we boys got some improvements. I remember well those days of the economic crisis when the government program called WPA was the only source of income. Dad earned $1 a day.

I remember the period in 1929 when I was a four year old and earned my first wages. It was 10 cents an hour. I worked 4 hours and I received my first check of forty cents. The family moved to Texas in 1939, and it seemed as though we were becoming stronger financially, but things began to change as Europe began war action with Hitler. The U.S. became supplier to other countries at war and the economy was edging up. By 1941, I was earning fifty cents an hour working for my dad. By 1942, the war actions made wages soar. I was adapting to the conditions and soon I bought my first car. It was a used 1937 Plymouth coupe. I decided that if I worked hard at whatever I could do, I would succeed. Maybe this was a farfetched idea. Nevertheless, I worked hard to succeed.

Life Is Difficult

My knowledge of what to do in the field of learning was related to what I learned from Dad. He was a carpenter and he taught each son how to follow his instruction. Because I dropped out of school when I finished the eighth grade, I was totally dependent upon the teaching of my father. He was an excellent person to show me all the tricks of the trade. I did not fathom the need to learn budget-control. I did remember that if you don't have much, you won't be able to spend much. In my early life, the banking rules and policies of operating a style of life by the credit card had not been established. It was not until I had married and followed the call of God to go to school that I began to learn the essentials of becoming a minister. I asked God to help me and He did.

From 1942, when I married, until 1951, I was continually involved in the "merry-go-round-circus style" of activity. The cycle was school, evangelize, and labor in the building trade. Then it would start all over again. Ten years of this style of activity gave me four years of schooling, two years of evangelizing, and four years as a building contractor.

Owning property became a dream for me. I was able to own a small four-room house with bath as the first home for my family. Along with that was an apartment on the same lot that became rental income. The year was 1949. During the next fifteen years, all of my efforts were channeled toward being the best minister, teacher, missionary, and pastor that I was capable of becoming. By that time, my finances were controlled by my assignment. I was not motivated to accept a position based upon how much it paid. Most often, the next assignment started out at a smaller salary than the one I had just finished.

Success Is Complicated

When 1965 arrived, I had been an active minister, student, builder, and one who had considered himself successful. Often I had used a phrase to express to others the reason for my "supposed success" in my work ethic. Because I had started in life as a builder and then became a minister, I would say in response to the "how or why" could I have achieved a level of achievement in such a short time that I was placed in an assignment on the basis of being paid as a preacher, and I was a builder at no cost.

In the course of the fourteen years, I helped as the engineer for the building of the Texas Campground, worked on the South Carolina Campground, built small homes in South Carolina, completed the total Mission Compound in Haiti, worked on the campground in Missouri, built a new church and parsonage in Webster Groves, Missouri, and a large sanctuary and Sunday school annex in Jackson, Mississippi.

During this same time, I served as the state youth director of Texas, the assistant pastor of Tremont Avenue Church in Greenville, South Carolina, missionary overseer of Haiti, pastor for eight years in St. Louis, Missouri, and one year in Jackson Mississippi.

Dreams or Dilemmas?

During this time in my life, I celebrated my fortieth birthday. I wondered what amount of effort was necessary to obtain financial security. I had given up a strong building business in Houston the year I helped complete the Texas Campground. Now, just because I believed I had achieved success, I was not saving any funds for my retirement.

My dilemma was conditioned by how difficult the economics of survival were. Two special people were my icons. My father-in-law, Reverend W. F. Ainsworth, had spent his entire life in ministry, but he had never saved any funds for retirement. He had left the Church of God organization in his midlife. Later, he returned and spent the balance of his ministry in the Church of God. However, he did not have the adequate number of years to fulfill the requirements under the retirement plan the church had provided. Subsequently, he moved into a small 24 x 24 square foot "cracker box" of a dwelling. He had no resources. I saw him beg for weekend appointments.

My dad retired in 1961 at age 65. Now four years later, he was facing the loss of his property because he could not meet the mortgage payment he had taken four years earlier. When I attempted to put together the puzzle that existed for these two family members, I shuddered at the thought of what would happen to me if I were to come to the age of 65 and have insufficient funds to live the balance of my days. I concluded that I might be able to live in a parsonage, provided by a congregation, but where would I go after my parsonage occupancy days were over?

Wisdom + Knowledge = Success

I negotiated a contract to purchase my father's property. I set aside a small plot where his home was situated and assumed the first mortgage obligation. I created a second mortgage with Dad and borrowed $7,500 as my down payment. I had created a $40,000 debt. I was obligated to maintain my personal budget and I had taken on a new debt. It took me fifteen years to pay off my mortgages, my bank loan, and keep my "head above water." I determined not wait to see whether I would be able to retire with ample financial resource, or be a pauper, as my father-in-law and my dad were. **BUT GOD foreknew** and **foresaw** my future. At the end of my fifteen-year budget crunch, my investment multiplied 500 percent. To God be the glory! I do not claim that wisdom or knowledge alone caused these events to happen, **but God** allowed the riches of these actions to supply my need.

I Remember . . .

In this chapter I have defined how my status developed in my personal affairs. Growing up as a boy during the Depression Era made me conscious of the meaning of living within my financial strata of debt to income. Since I did not come from a wealthy family, and since I saw both my father and my father-in-law collapse financially when they were in their sixties, I devised a plan to avoid their plight if at all possible

My brother, A. C. (Punk) was a prominent and wealthy person in Buffalo, Texas. Punk had moved to Buffalo in 1953 and bought land at $5 per acre. Owning over 1,500 acres, his land values were in the millions. First as a building contractor, Punk built many properties, and then he became involved as a real estate agent in Leon County, Texas. He would buy and sell a section at a time, develop it with lakes and roads, and sell it to anyone who wanted to ride the financial crest to prosperity.

I knew of his success. Punk was one of the most prominent business men in the county. I asked him if I could ride on his coattails. He volunteered to sell my small property in one- to ten-acre parcels. After providing for my mother and father's portion of land for their personal needs, I had 120 acres left in my tract.

Punk was in a position to select any and all prospects. Because he was developing 640-acre sections for wealthy prospects, he was also able to screen the buyers who only wanted a small tract. I did not have to screen any potential buyer of my parcels.

I asked Punk to arrange the sale to the buyer and stipulate that I would hold the mortgage note to be able to earn the mortgage note interest from a sale to the buyer. When President Jimmy Carter was in office, interest peaked at 22 percent. The rate of interest in 1980 had leveled off to 12 to 15 percent. As the seller, I was able to compound my return on my investment. I had bought the land for $200 per acre in 1965. I was now selling for $1,200 to $1,500 per acre depending on the tract size. What made these sales valuable was the fact that my property was on highway frontage. In the course of two years, I sold all of my land and held the mortgage notes.

During this two-year period, every time I accumulated $5,000 (interest and principal—about every three months), I would use the same amount to purchase rental property in Cleveland, Tennessee. It was the proposition of my broker to take $5,000 as a 10 percent down payment on a $50,000 property. The rate of inflation was high and I could gain a 10 percent growth on my new purchases in one year. I was able to purchase 35 units of rental property. On paper, my net worth greatly increased. I began to save and earn outside income from what God had permitted me to acquire in 1965 when I was determined to help my father and mother survive the final years of their lives. Dad lived to be eighty-eight, and Mom lived to age ninety-four. The parcel that I set aside for their home was theirs until they passed on. Only then, after I helped Mom and Dad survive, did I have the liberty to sell that last parcel (their house) twenty-four years later.

During these prosperity years, I was asked by my seventh brother, Dean, to join him in a joint-venture he had established in Houston. Dean had survived a debilitating health condition in early life. He contracted a variation of Lou Gerhig's disease. His feet and hands were seriously affected, but he continued to work as a contractor. I was invited to listen to his proposal. Dean had bought a number of acres just north of the Houston Airport and developed thirty-two warehouses on the plot. He intended to expand his warehouse project to include a manufacturing business on a portion of the acreage in this plot. In order to get into this manufacturing activity, he needed to remove himself from the warehouse portion of the business.

To gain his new business partner, a local Houston man who had a patent on preserving vegetables, needed some extra cash to develop his plan. The local banker had agreed to Dean's idea of expanding activity but determined that Dean must secure more working capital.

The property had been appraised with an MAI appraisal for $1 million. The bank had established with Dean that if he could acquire a new partner who was financially qualified, the banker would release Dean from his mortgage note. When I sent the banker my financial resume`, I was invited to become Dean's partner.

Another New Venture

I digress to explain a new episode that happened to me at this time. When I was a teenager in Houston, I made friends with our church family. I was married at age seventeen by a pastor across the city whose name was G. B. Byrne. His family became close to our family. Joe Byrne, one of Pastor Byrne's children was two years older than me. Joe had learned to fly an airplane. I was invited to become a passenger. Just north of Houston, as a teenager I acquired my desire to learn to fly a plane.

At age fifty-eight, while performing my duties of meeting and helping churches my office as overseer required, I made contact with an independent church in the northern area of Indianapolis. This church and its leadership wanted to join allegiance with the Church of God. From this development, I learned that the associate pastor of this church was also a pilot. Subsequently, I took lessons and became a licensed pilot of my own plane (purchased from my brother-in-law, Bill Ainsworth). With my pilot instructor as my copilot, we then flew to Houston to negotiate my new business venture with the bank who held my mortgage note. As I listened to the banker tell of Dean's new venture, he said that I, because of my financial net worth statement, could become Dean's new partner in Houston.

I was quite overwhelmed at the new proposal. Because of the $1 million value established by the appraisal of the MAI, I would not need any new cash. I signed my name on the mortgage note. The mortgage was for $625,000. The terms of my payments were at $8,000 per month principal and interest. Dean had rented all the warehouses and Martha, Dean's wife, was the bookkeeper for all rental income. I was advised that everything would run smoothly. Dean's expansion would continue because he was going to build a new building for the manufacturing plant.

When I bought the warehouse section, I was told by Dean that they were 100 percent occupied. When the occupants of the warehouses found that Dean had sold out to me, they began to vacate their leases. The occupancy dropped 40 percent. Lease income dropped because of vacancies and I had to borrow from my Cleveland accounts to sustain my negative budget in Houston.

The property was reevaluated with new MAI appraisals each year after I took possession. The new MAI was $1,200,000. During this decade, the U. S. economy was undergoing problems that related to the Savings and Loan Institution's policies. President Ronald Regan began procedures during his term in office to get control of the Savings and Loan system of lending and borrowing. The system that gave me a high value (stated value per Saving and Loan standards) was overvalued. I was headed for a financial calamity.

When I found my income stream to be insufficient to sustain my debt obligations, I determined to deed my property in Houston back to the bank for my unpaid mortgage balance. When the banker determined to prevent my giving him a quit-claim deed, he determined that a new MAI appraisal must be secured. When the new appraisal was submitted, the value of my property was declared to be $500,000. I asked who gave this new value at such a low price. When the banker gave his name, I was astounded. I told the banker that this was the same appraiser who had given a $1.2 million appraisal just the year before.

One year earlier my brother, A. C. (Punk), had been through a complex problem in his sale to a Houston buyer for some of his Buffalo property. When he found out how the banker was trying to manipulate my legal rights, he placed me in contact with a lawyer in Waco, Texas. According to Texas law, the small business owner could not be sued for default for less than 75 percent of a bona fide MAI appraisal. This meant that I would have a secure $900,000 status without liability of equity value. I would be allowed by Texas law to give a quit-claim deed and not be liable for any further debt on the Texas property. The bank could not file a judgment against me. The Texas law saved me from foreclosure judgment by the bank. However, in the five-year term with my Texas venture, my net worth diminished by $1 million. Again, I say praise the Lord who foreknows the way to help sustain me in all phases of my work ethic.

CHAPTER 20

COMPOUNDING PROBLEMS

"Wisdom and knowledge is granted...."
(2 Chronicles 1:12).

Being on the World Mission's Board from 1962 to 1966, I was privileged to speak in a number of camp meetings. In 1965 I had the opportunity to visit Indiana and speak at their camp meeting.

The overseer in Indiana at that time was David L. Lemons and the evening speaker was J. Frank Spivey. The camp meeting was convened in mid-central Indiana. Lakeside cottages and camping facilities made everyone feel that this was the right location for a real old-time camp meeting. I was excited to minister with a team I had come to admire many years earlier.

Just being in Indiana was exciting to me because I had been contacted a number of times while pastoring the church in St. Louis to see if I would be willing to exchange my church for one in Indianapolis. I chose not to leave St. Louis at that time. Now, sixteen years later, I had been assigned by the Executive Committee of the Church of God as the overseer of the great state of Indiana.

One year after I became overseer, I had a severe problem. The church had been moved from the central part in Indianapolis to a location called *Southwest Indy* (short for Indianapolis). This was the same church I had been asked to pastor sixteen years earlier. Pastor R. D. McKinney, their current pastor, had served on my Evangelism Board from Michigan days a decade earlier. He had learned how to finance his mortgage program from the "Bond Plan" I had instituted in Michigan. He had under built the building but overspent the bond plan for his mortgage. When the local church revolted on his continuing leadership, I was obligated to find a replacement.

I brought my son, Duane, to Indiana. Duane had been state youth director of Wisconsin and served as pastor of the Milwaukee Church. His marriage had broken almost simultaneously with this event in Indianapolis. With three teenage children, he moved in June 1981 into the parsonage and began a very expanding ministry.

Duane began preaching as a minister like me at an early age. At age thirty, he was ordained. Now at age thirty-eight, he is appointed to Indiana to work under me in a strong church. A divorce from his unfaithful wife became a crisis we all had to live through. Duane worked tirelessly for eighteen months to salvage his broken ministry. When his divorce decree was final, he felt relieved that his innocence had been established and his position in ministry saved.

When he concluded that he was eligible to find a legal new companion, he married in November 1982. The local congregation revolted. They defined him as being unworthy to continue as their pastor because he was now married the second time. At that time, our church prohibited a continued ordination for someone who has been divorced and remarried.

The harshest status of my ministerial authority became a mandate to me. My ordained minister son must be "unfrocked" (to deprive of the right to practice a profession). By the laws of our church system at that time, I was compelled to revoke his credentials and reduce his status to the rank of exhorter. This destroyed my son and he lost his position, status with the church, and credibility with others.

The injustice of law, which seems to be modified by whatever pressure prevails at a given time, came into effect the very next assembly. Our church polity became church law, and the revised rules now allow a divorced innocent minister to sustain his credentials. This law came into effect too late to help my son. He was politically judged to be in adultery, and therefore an infidel because of double marriage.

Greenwood Church of God

Going to Greenwood was an event that carried memories of my association with my long-time friend, Cecil Knight. It was Cecil who followed David Lemons as state overseer of Indiana. Cecil bought and developed the state office complex in Greenwood. The office was on the business plot of a large acreage. The state parsonage was three blocks away. At the primary cross street was the prominent Greenwood Church of God, one of the largest congregations of our churches. The parsonage was a very elegant two-story residence. It was so grand I felt as though I had been elevated to a status of riches.

The status of residence in a palace was offset by the condition of near bankruptcy in the state funds. The first month was conditioned by a meeting of the state council to determine how to survive financially. Unpaid mortgage debt on many church properties was almost more than the state could sustain.

When I called General Overseer Ray Hughes for financial help, I was told, "That's why we sent you to Indiana; we knew you would know how to bring the state funds back into the black."

The campground property had been sold in 1977, but the budget balance was very tight. Other properties had debt and were also in the complex basket of obligations. Many small congregations were unable to meet their obligations on their own church mortgage debt.

For the first two years, I was continually ministering to these small churches and attempting to resolve their financial predicaments. Along with these constant contacts, I was able to build a strong stance with the council. Having developed a sturdy program ten years earlier in Michigan with the bond program of financing, I was now placing these principles before the struggling churches of Indiana. It took two years for the state to begin to balance its budget and begin numerical and financial growth—both locally and at the state level.

A New Venture

Adapting to the routine of ministry, I found my time to be pushed to the limit. I now had officially ninety-six churches to care for and the relative issues of the leaders of those churches. At this time, I was recovering from the catastrophic aftermath of the New Jersey legal trials in Millville. What led up to and the events of the trial took more than a full year and a half to finalize.

Because I wanted to preserve all the data of those events; and because they were of a different kind of action than I had done heretofore, I determined to write and preserve it for future use. Having received my B. S. degree three years before this moment in my life's timetable, I thought the events of these years just past would be essential to my further educational status. I decided to write my master's thesis on "The Church—From Crisis and Crucible to Conquest." This writing defines the church from an anatomy and synthesis of the philosophy of government, polity, legal ethics, procedures, decisions, and conclusions; it is identified scripturally, theologically, materially, socially, and politically. I researched and reviewed the history of our church organization. With almost 200 pages of printed information, I defined and defended a position upon which I stand.

The Church of God is referred to as an organism as well as an organization. The congregations of believers are referred to from a local position and will be defined from every precept. Conditions that posed personal problems with judgment and decisions relating to justice are treated in the thesis. I write a short synopsis about these issues and define some of them as follows:

- How did the church come to its present position?
- How does the church determine its polity?
- How does the church define its status?
- How does the church regulate itself?
- How does the church treat its offenders?
- How can justice be equated with judgment?
- How can judicial review be interpreted fairly in an ecclesiastical frame of reference when the general opinion declared by many is forgive and forget?

- How does church policy relate to polity?
- Are there politics in the church?
- Are church leaders as ministers ever classified as politicians? Why?

The writing of this document is done for various reasons. My objectives in writing of these conditions, circumstances, and experiences, is to inform others who may read of my life's conflicts over the years and learn from them.

Having served as a minister, as of the time of my tenure in Indiana for forty years, I have drawn a conclusion that the issues which I set forth in this writing are necessary. I will identify conditions that brought my church from its beginning to the present through a variety of changes. Though change is an ever-present circumstance, there is a continuing relevance from issue to issue. I also believe that some of the experiences obtained within my tenure of pastoral and administrative assignments have granted me the right to express my opinion in these matters.

Intertwining Activity

When the financial problems of the state office were put into the plan for financial solvency, I felt compelled to obtain a real estate broker who would be able to perform our council's strategy. Even though I knew how to buy and sell real estate, I realized that every state has a probable variation of realty law. Since a church was paying its mortgage loan to a local financial institution, I considered a safety measure would be to deal with a bona fide realtor in negotiating either a sale of property or a refinance. That person who became my specialist was Ron Fisher. Ron Fisher through listing agreements, enforceable legal documents, was employed by the Church of God in Indiana to sell a number of properties during a period of more than three years while I was overseer. In this sense, Mr. Fisher was the agent of the Church of God legally employed to render a particular service for a contracted and negotiated fee. Consequently, Mr. Fisher developed a relationship with the Church of God in a continuing business position. While Fisher wanted to enter into a partnership with the Indiana Church of God, I, as overseer, with state council consent, determined it would not be in our best interest to permit such an arrangement.

Time and time again, the church administration had tried to find congregations—both independent and organizationally—regulated to buy our church property on 38th Street. Our local congregation at that address had failed to survive over the years.

The church leaders thought that the location ought to be sustained for church use; yet, each time financial limitations blocked the sale. Subsequently, Mr. Fisher negotiated a contract to be the buyer of the parcel known as the 38th Street Property. He executed a note with stipulations that he would pay certain interest over a four-year term. This would permit his having a basis for a vested interest without having to have his actions reviewed by the state council. This would further expedite his liberties to make a sale to any prospective client, make a profit for himself, and pay us (Indiana State Office) the equity we had in the property.

The state council came to believe that much of Mr. Fisher's actions were not only speculative, but often inconclusive and with little concrete evidence of being able to perform. In due process of time, after numerous proposed sales to prospective buyers, all of which failed to consummate, Mr. Fisher came up with the final client. Chi Chi Restaurants finally consummated a deal with the joint effort of the state office. By the time of the Chi Chi sale, Mr. Fisher had a vested position in the property since we had compelled him, by contractual obligation, to begin paying the stipulations of his purchase of the 38th Street property.

It was determined not to be in the best interest of the Church of God to vest our position totally in Mr. Fisher's hands relating to the property at 38th Street. Two years earlier than the date of the closing of this sale, the state council, sensing the long drawn-out timeframe it took to bring the other sales to final disposition, granted me as overseer the privilege and powers necessary to act for and in the best interest of the Church of God to attend to any and all the details of any transaction.

Because of the facts that the property would not be sold for church use, it was concluded that necessary action would be taken to get the property rezoned. When Mr. Fisher's client became interested, it was necessary to pursue all the regulatory rules for rezoning this property. The church was on a residential classification with nonconforming use allowed. To have the parcel zoned commercial would perhaps double the asking price of a sale and multiply our equity by 400 to 500 percent over the amount we would receive to sell to a congregation with continuing church use.

It took almost two years to obtain the zoning approval from the Indianapolis Zoning Board. With this condition, we had to satisfy not only the pending buyer but also the holder of the original mortgage note. Here was a part of the problems we had to resolve. City Hall would only consider any proposal for rezoning if the sellers and the buyer would jointly file for rezoning. By this process, it was determined that we could get our equity (total of $80,000 loaned to Fisher), pay the Church of Christ their first mortgage note in excess of $150,000, and have the balance of the purchase money $70,000 for evangelism in Indiana.

One of the Chi Chi requirements in obtaining their parcel was that final topography be suitable for their building. Consent had to be obtained from the Church of Christ, holder of the original mortgage to grant Chi Chi this option. The Church of Christ would not allow the demolition of the building since this would minimize the value of their equity in their mortgage. Only if the building should be removed to another location could it be considered feasible that the equity values be sustained to protect the Church of Christ. Consequently, the Church of God found it necessary to arrange with Mr. Fisher the process to fulfill all these contingencies.

Since Fisher did not have the funds to accomplish this, the state council agreed to loan Ron Fisher $40,000 for moving this building and to rehab it on a parcel on High School Road. This tract was less than one-half mile away. Notes with Fisher were negotiated to secure the Church of God in their equity in that transaction. Concurrently, a $10,000 loan was made to Fisher to acquire a parcel on 3808 Lawndale. This parcel would permit ingress and egress to the Chi Chi Restaurant parcel. Indianapolis zoning requirements mandated this action. Fisher could not sustain all his obligations. Ten months after he bought the Lawndale property, I, through a personal loan, acquired the Lawndale parcel after the ingress, egress portion had been titled to the commercial tract. I later sold the Lawndale parcel.

The reasons and the purpose for which we held out on the matter of separating the state office from this business position was based on the fact that I would have my term ended as overseer with the probability of outstanding contingencies unresolved between the Church of God and Fisher at my departure from Indiana. Fearing Mr. Fisher's inability to fulfill his often proposed dreams, we determined through past experiences of nonperformance that he might be unable to accomplish any proposal which the Church of God might be joint ventured in. We resolved that the state office should not have to be affected by that probability. Subsequent complications and default on note and interest payments by Fisher on these last negotiations between the state office and Fisher have proven me right.

When I came to Indiana in 1980 as overseer, I spent two years of that assignment tying together various and sundry issues of a virtually bankrupt system of the state organization. Upon leaving the state office in 1984, over $513,000 dollars in assets receivable were shown from the national auditor, Dudley Pyeatt's annual audit report of the state funds. Along with these duties came the normal and continuing activities of the care of the churches.

CHAPTER 21

TRANSITION

"Moreover it is required . . . that a man be found faithful" (1 Corinthians 4:2).

Upon leaving state overseer work, I was appointed by the Executive Committee as pastor of the Princeton, West Virginia, Church of God. This church was one of the large congregations in the state where prominent church leaders had served as pastor. However, since the local leaders of the church congregation had not been given the opportunity to express their desire for a pastor after their pastor was promoted to a state level assignment, I was not greeted with open arms. Since I was a "stranger" to them and because I was not a citizen of their state of West Virginia in my prior ministry, I had a difficult time being accepted.

Concurrent with my new pastor position, I was appointed as a member of the school board of the Northwest Bible School in Minot, North Dakota. This position was a new activity for me. I had served on state boards as a state councilor in every state where I had previously ministered. This was the first time I was privileged to work on a school board. After two years, I became the chairman of that board.

Locally, I was usually a persuasive person and when I found that the Princeton Church of God wanted to expand their property acquisition of a new location, I tried to take action to accomplish this objective. It didn't go well, and I did not survive but one year as their leader. The bounce from one place to somewhere else was conditioned by my placement, ultimately, to the state of Alabama.

I came to Lott Road Church in Mobile, Alabama in 1985. I began a concentrated pattern of adapting in the best manner I knew how. I was not willing to be pushed out of my new placement.

My Physical Downfall

I had begun to have health problems when I was in West Virginia. I had not been in Alabama but just a couple of months when I underwent a severe kidney-stone problem. I went to the hospital near midnight unable to bear the severe pain of the kidney stone. The doctor crushed the stone and I found relief. When I asked the doctor to give me a further review of my hemorrhoid condition, I was given a shock. I was told that I had colon cancer.

My nurse at Springhill Hospital in Mobile gave me a report that frightened me. Being the widow of a minister, she shocked me with these words: "Preacher, if you don't think this report is serious, just wait six months and then go pick out your tombstone." I now had to decide what I should do. The next month as I was preparing for a devotional subject for a prayer conference, past midnight I opened my Bible to Psalm 118. When I began reading I was ecstatic when I read the words of verse 17: "I shall not die, but live, and declare the works of the Lord."

I now knew my condition was serious. I had treated my hemorrhoid condition for years with creams to relieve the pain that was always there. Though I had presumed my pain to be treatable, it was not. My doctor's prognosis was clearly stated. It was surgery or else. Three months later in February 1986, I had eighteen inches of my colon removed. Because of the severity of the radical surgery, I was given a colostomy.

I found the congregation at Lott Road to be a very strong and wonderful group of people. Many great Church of God leaders had been the "shepherd" to these fine folk. They had a large property acreage and a great location on one of the state highways that led into Mississippi. They had built a large gymnasium and classroom building on their land, but their sanctuary needed to be much larger.

The location for a new sanctuary was to be in front of and connected to the gym. I was thrilled with the decisions already defined by the local church. The congregation had many members who were skilled in the field of construction. The Lott Road Church had existed at this location for more than twenty years. Now they were excited over the possibility of a new sanctuary.

Financial calculations became my first order of activity. The sanctuary was to be designed with a capacity seating of five hundred. A balcony seating would provide for overflow accommodations when the needs occurred. It was necessary to secure an architect who would know how to design and make all the specifications fit the city code requirements. This mandated an organized and complete project package for us to reach our objectives. The projected costs would be well over one-half million dollars. The church began a capital fund drive to establish their capability to maintain a proper debt to income ratio in order to complete this new building.

About this time I had just recovered from my surgery and was learning how to deal with my radical new digestive procedure. It took me quite a number of weeks with my medical technician to learn how to live with a colostomy. I not only faced this physical problem, I also had to learn how to fit them into my pastoral duties. I found the people of South Alabama very friendly and pleasant. My work was exciting at the Lott Road Church of God. The members had been kind and supportive during my surgery. I was reminded of the way I had worked with the local congregation in St. Louis, Missouri, thirty years earlier.

Having finished my executive-level work, I determined to begin to phase into my years toward retirement. After all, I was now sixty-two years old and I realized that in three more years, I would become eligible for my Social Security benefits.

Since Virgie and I would need a home of our own, a parsonage would not be my place of retired living. I began to look for an area that appealed to Virgie and me. Living in Mobile, I scouted the territory within a twenty-five-mile radius. I found Daphne, Alabama, to be the ideal place. A prominent builder of homes in the area had begun the construction of a condominium complex one block off the main street. This retirement complex was only one-half mile overlooking Mobile Bay. It was designed to be twelve stories high. I negotiated to buy a condo on the fifth floor. Construction had just begun on the ground floor when I made my decision to purchase.

Everything seemed to be going well until I heard from the executive level of leadership. I was informed that Indiana problems I thought were settled had now exploded!

In the next few months, I was overwhelmed at the way everything was unraveling. I was compelled to enter into an attempt to "close the book" on the whole Indiana issue. The conditions and the finality of this episode are dealt with in the following chapter.

At the same time the Indiana events were unfolding, I was given my medical doctor's new advice. His comments were alarming. He said, "Find some place to enjoy your last days." I had taken action six months earlier to respond to my nurse who said, "Preacher, if you don't think this is serious, wait six months and then pick out your tombstone."

Because my condo in Daphne was not yet completed for occupancy, I was pressed to search for an alternative. When I left Hawaii in 1977 to accept my New Jersey appointment, I could not sell my condo in Mililani Town. It had been rented for ten years. I decided very quickly that our best option was to move back to my condo in Hawaii to enjoy my last days.

CHAPTER 22

A NEW PROBLEM

"Wisdom is the principal thing; therefore get wisdom; and with thy getting get understanding" (Proverbs 4:7).

After leaving my Indiana assignment, I was surprised at the way my successor responded with his attempts to force a conclusion to financial matters relating to the Chi Chi transaction. When I left Indiana in August 1984, I left a detailed report of the status of everything the incoming overseer would need to know. This report included information relative to the churches, the leaders, financial reports, and the balance sheet of the state funds, accounts payable and accounts receivable.

After the new overseer Dennis McGuire was assigned, I called him to volunteer any information he might need as it related to the notes owed to the state funds by Ron Fisher—noting that Fisher's accounts were delinquent. I further informed Brother McGuire of the issues as they related to the 38th Street sale.

Brother McGuire did not ask me for any information. Months later, I was informed by a call from the state overseer that he was going to sue Ron Fisher in order to force a settlement for his debts to the state funds of Indiana. I volunteered to contact Fisher on behalf of McGuire. Later, I was informed that McGuire and Fisher had a confrontation in the lawyer's office in downtown Indianapolis and that an impasse had occurred and all communication between the parties had ceased.

A lawsuit was instituted by the law office of John P Wilson, legal counsel for the Indiana Church of God. The suit was filed against Ron Fisher for the debt owed to the state funds of the Church of God. When the suit came before the court in Indianapolis, the judge hearing the case declined to grant the Church of God the judgment sought for in its civil suit. Further information received revealed an injunction requested by Mr. Fisher to have the judgment sought by the Church of God set aside was deferred until the discrepancies should be determined between the parties.

As a result of Mr. Fisher's unwillingness or possible inability to fulfill the terms of his notes through this civil process, he attempted to cloud the court's understanding of all that preceded as well as that which followed my departure from Indiana. It was assumed that Mr. Wilson, the state office's legal counsel in this matter was being compelled by the court to bring a reasonable answer to the long sought-for decision in this case.

It must be remembered that I began using Ron Fisher for sales and purchases, beginning 1981, my first year in Indiana. Now five years later, 1986, and two years after my tenure in Indiana was over, this lawsuit between Fisher and the Church of God in Indiana was being heard by a court that denies the judgment sought and asks for new data.

Lawyer Wilson attempted to explain and expand the data in the renewed case. Instead of helping the Church of God, the procedure against Fisher subsequently brought a counter claim against the state office and me. Lawyer

Wilson alleged a fiduciary irregularity against me because of my purchase of the Lawndale property from Fisher. I bought Lawndale from Fisher ten months after the Chi Chi sale was completed.

When the case between the Church of God and Fisher became jammed and unsettled, I was contacted about the whole matter. I met with the Indiana State Council and overseer just two months before McGuire's tenure was up. McGuire was assigned to Texas, and Robert Herrin came to Indiana as overseer in 1986.

While I was in the presence of the overseer and his council, I went over all the data that related to the Fisher interaction as the agent in the realty area. Overseer McGuire stated that I had satisfactorily identified the facts and that everything, as stated in that meeting was clear and satisfactory. However, after Herrin came to the state and the Fisher note liability had not been resolved, I learned by a letter from the general overseer that I was being subjected to a fiduciary charge in these matters.

I was given a directive to finalize a settlement with the state of Indiana. From the time of that directive, it took over a year to bring the issues to all parties to an understanding of my position in the case. From the time of my departure from Indiana until the issue of the document clearing me of my alleged fiduciary accountability was three years. No judgment was rendered against me. What monetary settlement received by the Indiana Church of God is not known by me.

It was reported that Fisher declared bankruptcy and therefore no money settlement came to the church funds. It was very difficult for me to overcome the accusations, allegations, and false reports placed against me.

Emotionally, I was extremely perplexed about how this whole matter was handled.

I carried the proverbial "chip on my shoulder" for years because of how and why the officials of the church tried to "destroy me politically." It was alleged that "Fisher was bankrupt but Heil had wealth" and therefore, I should have to pay the Church of God of Indiana Fisher's obligation of $140,000.

Financial Strength

I use a quotation from the thesis I wrote five years prior to this episode. "If authority is misused and polity or law is misapplied, then justice has been misappropriated, and judgment is a mistake." I show that regardless of the events noted in this chapter during my tenure in Indiana, I was able to bring the Church of God back into solvency and financial strength. I was accused of fiduciary irregularity as it related to finances. Even though the Chi Chi sale, as agreed by the council two years prior to final approval was accepted at $200,000, I finalized the sale at $300,000.

By the actions of my successor, I was alleged to have been in a partnership position with Mr. Fisher. I was not! I was devastated by the accusations of my peers. I concluded that Lawyer Wilson, who had served as my personal counsel, as well as counsel for the state office, had violated the ethics of revealing my financial net worth. It was reported that in divulging my personal net worth and Wilson's statement that since Fisher was bankrupt, the state office should file action to recover the assets from the Fisher note from me.

I realized that with this kind of alleged action against me, the future probability of being assigned to any future appointment in the Church of God was destroyed. This again is where my axiom comes into play in defining this statement, "If authority is misused, and polity or law is misapplied, then justice has been misappropriated, and judgment is a mistake." I lost hope in my future in the Church of God. I held a grudge against those who misinterpreted my efforts and tried to hold me accountable for wrong-doing in my work ethic in Indiana.

When I went back to Indiana after Virgie's passing, I attended a camp meeting in Indianapolis in 1993. After the night service, I spoke to the evening speaker, Brother McGuire, and asked for forgiveness for my anger against the system and the people who had destroyed me. After hearing my appeal for forgiveness, Brother McGuire said to me, "I made a mistake." He did not make any further comments to me nor did I ever hear from him again about the event which is now my personal history.

CHAPTER 23

LEGAL REVIEW

"Doth God pervert judgment? or doth the Almighty pervert justice?" (Job 8:3).

"Behold God will not cast away a perfect man, neither will he help the evil doers" (Job 8:20).

In attempting to resolve some grave issues, I'm continuing in this chapter to deviate from my former style of writing in chapter 22. Do you think this scripture above would apply to me or anyone, who like me, is in leadership, authority, and responsibility? My purview follows.

Judicial Polity

The process of dealing with a problem is knowing what the issue is and determining how to go about dealing with it. It has always been my observation that when a problem prevails, it should not be "covered up" as the proverbial saying goes. To deal with a problem often requires a delving into all of the issues or circumstances in order to decide how to properly deal with it and settle the issue.

In church work, I have been challenged by the variety of problems that have existed during the 100-plus years of our organization's history. Being a person who has always loved history, when I was a student I came to realize the magnitude of it. Learning for me in early years of my life was by studying and experience. As a young man, I realized the importance of living a good life before the public and before the Lord who called me to preach the Gospel. I did not want to have a mark against my character or my reputation. To this end, I always have determined to keep every reference open for review.

As I have said, during my early years of growing up, I learned by studying and by experience. In later years of leadership of my life, I have come to realize that my life is subject to review by anyone and everyone with whom I have been associated. It has always been my desire to perform every task so that I shall have unquestionable acceptance by whomever reviews my work.

When the problem developed in New Jersey, I was compelled by the situation to maintain the status of my position and show fairness toward everyone with whom I had responsibility. The circumstances between the leader of the local church and me caused a civil lawsuit to be initiated. It took seven and one-half months of civil court action before the decision was rendered by the court in favor of the New Jersey Church of God. I believe in a judicial method functioning in church work. My personal responsibility in determining and sustaining the New Jersey church's status was mandated by my superior leaders. To this end, I was obligated to be at the local Church of God every service schedule. I had only one month from the end of the civil trial until my tenure as overseer of New Jersey was finished.

I was appointed in August 1980 to be the state overseer of Indiana. The previous chapter reveals the magnitude of issues and problems of my Indiana assignment.

In my second year of duty in Indiana, I concluded that the problem of my New Jersey years needed to be totally recorded for posterity. I decided the only way to properly identify all the issues, events, conditions, and decisions would best be done in the form of a book. I decided to write a thesis for my Master's Degree and hoped to keep those records so a complete recollection and review would be available to whoever was interested. My thesis was titled "THE CHURCH From Crisis and Crucible to Conquest." This writing included many facets of review, namely, Church of God philosophy of government, polity, legal ethics, procedure, decisions, and conclusions. To those who would choose to read this work, a copy is available in the Lee University library in Cleveland, Tennessee.

Perhaps the biggest issue that is to be confronted in stating my position on this subject is summed up in the word *change*. I looked up the meaning of the word. The dictionary says change is relevant to any system from beginning to end. It must be determined from a beginning point and reviewed from there until an end is fixed for evaluation. The church as I have come to know it has been one of continuing change. I will begin my review of issues that have occurred in the church.

The Church of God organization which I joined as a teenager in 1934 was a tightly controlled church with a Presbyterian, Episcopal-type government. Leadership authority was delegated to the general overseer and the elected council. The operation of its leadership maintained strong authority. Theology is biblically based with rules, regulations, and polity tightly controlled. Many rules that controlled the church, made it by classification, a church of extreme conservatism.

Over the course of the seventy-eight years I have been associated with our Church of God organization, I have found its theology to be unchanged. Biblically, the Declaration of Faith, ratified in 1948 by the General Assembly, has not had one jot nor tittle of modification. However, the polity of the church has become liberal in classifying the rules of demeanor. With revisions and codifying of laws, bylaws, polity, and so forth, the scope of church procedure has grown over the decades. Laws are created to be observed. How the church performs this action leads me to another view.

Ethics and Justice

Ethics by definition is the discipline dealing with what is good or bad and with moral duty and obligation. Stated another way, ethics involves the principles and disciplines by which an individual's conduct is governed. If it is presumed that a decision is declared to be unethical, there must be fair process to deal with the issue.

What is the price of justice? Sometimes it is the price of judgment. While a student in my second year at B. T. S., my professor who taught me these principles further stated, "Any law without a penalty is a joke." To defend these principles, I found that my position in determining what was ethical and just often had to have a verdict of judgment before the case could be closed. One of the primary rules to be observed in meting out justice is that one must not be inconsistent with ethical standards and judicial procedures. I found my position being reviewed often by others who questioned whether I had conducted the business of the church according to these precepts.

Because of my ridged standard for doing the church business according to these rules, I was aware that I would be judged by the same law. I further analyzed by the law of logic an axiom that I therefore created: If authority is misused and polity or law is misapplied, then justice has been misappropriated, and judgment is a mistake.

I have concluded by the principles of the rules upon which I served in my leadership roles, that I will be subject to the evaluations gleaned thereby. When I look back, I find that the complexities of my experiences have led me through some very trying times. I have been affected by these events and issues that have placed my judgment in question. But the same God who gave me a knowledge of events that would happen to Virgie months before they occurred is the same God who has, in His way and in His time, brought me through all of my other complex problems.

CHAPTER 24

DESTINY ADJUSTMENTS

" . . . for there is a time there for every purpose and for every work" (Ecclesiastes 3:17).

Being assigned to pastor in Alabama was an experience I was happy to accept. I had always worked in the outlying regions of our nation. Appointment to one of the southeastern states allowed me to find fellowship with a very large number of ministers in our state meetings. I was now considered to be an Alabamian. I wanted to finish my time of ministry in this beautiful state. After my sickness with kidney stones was over, an operation for colon cancer seemed to set my destiny to a new lifestyle. I determined to live by God's rules and adapt to whatever must be for as long as He would permit. I enjoyed my fellowship with ministers and laity. When the doctor implied a limited lifespan, we decided to move back to Hawaii.

Back in Hawaii

Ten years had passed since we left Hawaii. This fabulous location in Mililani Town had been our home while I was assigned to the Ministry to the Military. I did not know how I was going to meet my budget. No job offers awaited me. The only thing I was sure of was that I had a place to live. We arrived in Mililani Town in the fall of 1987. My brother, L.E. (Ed), had moved to Hawaii in 1980 to begin a business. He and Letha had finished their mission work in Japan in 1965. Ed's intent was to develop a new business with the A.L. Williams Insurance Company. This firm had begun in Georgia in the 1970 decade. Ed had begun his business with A.L. Williams in 1980. I came back to Hawaii in 1987. I had no commitment to be involved job wise with anyone. The only thing I thought to be important was the emphasis by the doctor to "find some place to enjoy my last days."

I was happy to reunite with family. Because Ed and I had been in ministry since our teen years, it was now a new venture to just be family in our weekly activities. I had not been in Hawaii very long when Ed asked me to join his business. I was to be employed as an insurance salesman. Further, I was asked to be Ed's office manager. Salary in his business was based on a portion of the insurance premium on the policies written. Since I was "a new person on the block," I certainly didn't know anyone who would be a customer for insurance. I quickly accepted the idea of just becoming his office manager. By that time, Ed had over 200 people under his jurisdiction. My title seemed to be excellent, but the problem I had related to my lack of computer knowledge. Ed said, "There is the computer—go to work." Fear took over. I had never tried to do one thing on the computer until that time.

Back to Pastoral Work

One month later, I was called by the state overseer who informed me that a local church in Honolulu needed a pastor. While I could not fathom how to meet my financial needs, God had, again, opened the door for my security in sustaining a budget.

The Coolidge Street Church had been established as a mission in the late 1940s. The church was within two miles of the famous Waikiki Beach. I had been aware of this wonderful "mother" church of all the Hawaiian church work, and I felt honored to be appointed as pastor. Back in the decade of the Coolidge Street church's establishment, there was no foresight relating to expansion or parking. Consequently, the building on the property covered the lot with no space left to expand. When investigations were made about buying more land, we found the price of a 50 X 120 foot lot to be $1,000,000. The congregation of the Coolidge Church was totally native Hawaiian. It was wonderful to be able to serve this fine group of people. However, because they were locally native, there was no probability of their being able to buy more land.

Adapting to this new style of activity was pleasant even though there was little probability of financial security from either of my two assignments. I determined I would not try to push to find wealth but rather to find happiness for my "last days." Some of the most pleasant experiences came from serving as guide with people who came for a "Hawaiian vacation" in the exciting places that made Hawaii famous. I would have them minister to my beautiful native group, and we would reminisce about friendship times.

Special Recognition

After becoming an "adopted Hawaiian" because of my being the pastor of the Coolidge Street Church in Honolulu, I found a very special emphasis from the Service men's Division. During their annual retreat they honored me.

Having served in my military-related assignment three years from 1974-1977, I was transferred to my overseer assignment in New Jersey by an instantaneous action (see end of chapter 17).

Now that I have returned to Hawaii eleven years later, these people who make up such a great division of the Hawaiian work desired to give me special recognition for my past position as servicemen's director to the military.

During the servicemen's retreat at the Aiea Servicemen's Center in June of 1988, I was given an honor that is beyond the highest recognition I could have ever imagined. I was presented the flag that flew from the USS ARIZONA flagpole mounted on that battleship's mainmast. With the flag, I was honored with a "Certificate of Flag Presentation." The full document is printed below.

Certificate of Flag Presentation

Ship Seal — **USS Arizona**

to

REVEREND WAYNE HEIL

In tribute to the American fighting men killed during the attack on Pearl Harbor, the national ensign is flown daily over the sunken battleship USS ARIZONA in its resting place in 38 feet of water at the bottom of Pearl Harbor.

The battleship is no longer in commission, having been stricken from the active list in 1942, but the Secretary of the Navy has granted special permission to fly the United States Flag over the ship in memory of the brave men killed during the attack on Pearl Harbor on December 7, 1941.

The flag is flown from 8 a.m. to sunset. It appears to fly from the USS Arizona Memorial but in fact does not touch any part of the memorial, which spans the sunken hull of the battleship. The flag is flown from a flagpole mounted on the battleship's mainmast, which is still visible above the water.

The United States Flag accompanying this certificate was raised and lowered from this flagpole on ___19 JUNE 1988 at 1738___.

Signed and authenticated this date, ___20 JUNE 1988___.

WILLIAM K. DICKINSON
National Park Service
Superintendent
USS Arizona Memorial

R. T. REIMANN
Rear Admiral, U.S. Navy
Commander
Pearl Harbor Naval Base

I cannot find appropriate words to express my feelings when I received this honor. Again, I express my feelings by writing the following.

The National Park Service Superintendent of the USS ARIZONA Memorial, William K. Dickinson, and Rear Admiral, U S Navy Commander—Pearl Harbor Naval Base, R. T. Reimann, the highest authority of this military memorial—presented me with a tribute for which I am forever humbled and thankful. To be given the high honor of receiving the flag that flew over the USS ARIZONA at Pearl Harbor, Hawaii, and a certificate from the USS ARIZONA authorities overwhelms me. Thank you, military and memorial authorities, and thank you servicemen and women for honoring me.

More Health Problems

Four years earlier, after the death of her father, in two weeks, Virgie lost her memory. But after 30 days of shock treatment, and with the help of doctors and the wonderful God we serve, she had full mental recovery. With my colon surgery three years later, we found it hard to adapt to a normal life. So Virgie and I took a trip to Europe.

Many locations became interesting to us. We wanted to travel by bus or train to see as many places as we could at the most moderate cost. In Switzerland a visit to a mountaintop location created a major problem for Virgie. Sightseeing at the mapped locations was routine, but we took the wrong path to return to the cable car for departure, and the distance around the mountaintop was almost a mile. Virgie's ability to walk was limited. She ultimately told me she could walk no further. I picked her up, put her on my back, and walked back to the cable car building. It was almost a half mile. We vowed never again to take a wrong path.

During this period of our life, both of us recognized that our physical limitations mandated that we adjust to a less strenuous routine of activity. We knew that we could not continue a fast-paced activity or a pressured schedule.

Ed had been diagnosed as having Parkinson's problems. After a long period of limited ability and trying to sustain the travel schedules his business demanded, he decided to move back to the mainland for the convenience of his business routine. With Ed knowing that I had bought my condo earlier in Daphne, he was quick to respond to a letter I received about a new development there.

Alabama Bound

The Loma Alta Towers was a twelve-story condominium complex. Before the builder had completed the building, he went bankrupt. The units of the complex were being put up for auction. Since I had bought my unit on a preconstruction date, I was notified of the pending auction. Ed was very much interested in acquiring a unit. He had heard me speak of the fabulous locale next to Mobile Bay. I was given airfare and Ed asked me to be at the auction and give a bid to purchase a unit for him and Letha.

I had never bought property before by auction bid. The only knowledge I had was based on the fact that I knew the preconstruction prices of the units as advertised by the builder. After all, I had been a reputable, licensed salesperson for these units three years earlier. Originally, the top floor units were priced at $200,000 dollars. I had bought my fifth floor unit #503 three years earlier and paid $174,500 for it. When the possible buyers assembled, we were eager to see where the auctioneer would begin pricing a unit for bid. Ed had asked me to bid on a twelfth-floor unit with a view facing south.

When the bidding started, I was the first to offer a bid. When the bidding stopped, my price of $147,500 set the benchmark for all sales. This unit was on the top floor. Subsequently, all other bids never exceeded the price I gave to buy the unit for Ed. The excitement prevailed and the buyers capitalized on a very low-priced market. When bidding was pursued for third-floor purchases, I bought unit 204 for $104,500. My purpose in buying this unit was because I felt that I had bought a bargain that I would be able to sell for a profit some time later. When all units were sold, some purchasers had bought units for under $100,000.

This action was finalized and Ed and Letha became residents of Alabama in the summer of 1992. Carrying on his A.L. Williams business was now expedited from a much closer proximity to the Atlanta office.

Mililani Town

When I first came to Hawaii in 1974 to fill my assignment in the Ministry to the Military, I searched for the most reasonable location to purchase a residence. The community called *Mililani Town* was ten miles from Pearl Harbor. I considered ten miles of local travel to my office relatively easy, since all my other travel to the Asian stations had been by air. The location of our residence was within the hub of the military complexes. Purchasing our condo in 1975 for $54,500 allowed me a mortgage for which I qualified. Twelve years later, we were able to move back to this wonderful community.

The location for residency was ideal; however, since I became Ed's office manager in downtown Honolulu and also pastor of the Coolidge Street Church in midtown Honolulu, my travel from home to work and church was compounded by heavy traffic as well as the distance of twenty miles each way.

The only satisfaction I had was in the fact that moving to Hawaii again in 1987 was feasible by having retained my residence in Mililani Town. Maintaining the condo as a rental unit for ten years allowed me to accelerate the mortgage pay-off.

By the time we moved back, the value of our property doubled from the amount we had paid. We lived in a complex with more than seventy residential units on the golf course. To play golf was convenient, and our price in 1974 to play eighteen holes was $6. The Mililani golf course was purchased by Japanese investors because of its beautiful layout and proximity to military bases nearby. The price of golf at Mililani Town for eighteen holes in 1987 was $65 per game, and residents did not get priority tee-times. We had to wait until three o'clock for tee-time.

By 1989 the Japanese were accelerating purchases of property in key areas of the world. One of these areas was Hawaii. In one year, our property values doubled again. I felt blessed to have this wonderful condo as my financial nest-egg after having lost so much of my personal equity in the Houston business just two years earlier.

Family Reunion

With Ed and Letha moving back to the mainland, the adjustments to living alone without our kinsfolk was a problem for us. Virgie was having more problems with her heart. In just four weeks, we would be traveling to the mainland to attend the General Assembly in New Orleans. We had made our plans to have a family reunion in Buffalo, but Virgie was unable to be with all of our Heil family. She was bedfast for the week. When we arrived in New Orleans, she had to travel from the hotel to the General Assembly floor at the coliseum in a wheelchair.

When the General Assembly was over and we arrived back home, we knew we must find a place back in the mainland for our residency. Virgie was unable to climb the stairs from the carport to our living area. This is the same kind of problem she faced in 1976 before her third heart surgery. So in 1992, we decided to move back to the mainland.

A realtor I located in Mililani Town was a person who had grown up in the orphanage at Cleveland, Tennessee. Because of his church affiliation as a child, it was easy for us to schedule a trip again to see if he could find us a location to buy. Because he had so much knowledge of the property available in that area, we began weekly review with him to find the best location at the right price.

Three months went by before we settled on what to do. The location offered was a beautiful property just four miles west of Cleveland, Tennessee, but the house had stairs. Therefore, it was a no-buy. We thought the best possibility was to be near family, so we drove to Indianapolis to spend some time with Duane and Sandy.

On arriving, I began to search the newspapers for a place near Duane. In Fishers, Indiana, a town bordering Indianapolis, I found an ideal location at a right price. The seller was offering his home and there was no agent between seller and buyer. I made an offer and it was accepted. Virgie was happy. The house was one block off the major business street. This event climaxed the week of Thanksgiving. We were so thankful that we didn't know quite how to react and celebrate our next move. Thanksgiving dinner was over and we thought we would settle down. Virgie collapsed again.

What Next?

I knew it was an absolute necessity for us to get back home to her doctors in Hawaii. We arrived home and Virgie was admitted to the hospital. God's direction and help to allow her to get medical help through four open-heart mitral valve surgeries from 1966 to 1983 was now about to come to an end. One week after our decision to move back to Indiana, Virgie passed on to the beautiful paradise of God.

On December 1, 1992, I had to begin thinking of *what next*? The funeral arrangements were too complex to decide for a local Hawaii funeral. After all, we had no family left in Hawaii and the price of burial arrangements were so expensive. I finalized everything quickly. I had a local service at Coolidge Street Church and another one in Pasadena, Texas, since this was where all of her family resided. The final destination was a plot in Fishers, Indiana, just two miles from the place Virgie had chosen to be her home.

Leaving Hawaii

When I arrived back in Hawaii from the funeral, I had only one alternative: I determined to resign my church and relocate back in Indiana. I informed my overseer, Orville Hagan, that I would give the church to him to appoint a new leader when I sold my home in Mililani Town.

It took six months for a sale to be made. The price of the sale brought four times the price I paid for the unit seventeen years earlier. In all this I conclude again and again, that God foreknew what the beginning issues of my Hawaii venture were and He also knew the end of my time there. Can anybody question that God is in control of life? Can anyone argue that God knows how to design, determine, direct, and decide what will be our pattern of life? He not only foreknew where our path would lead, He also knew the complex issues we would encounter, and He would see that the end of all the events were far better than the beginning.

When the condo was sold, I wrote my overseer and said, "I have decided to retire." I was going to finish the assignment as pastor of a wonderful church. I forgot to calculate that, because of resigning without a weekly salary, my budget for living must still be determined. With the sale of my condo, I realized that the amount of my sale price would not last indefinitely. After all, at age sixty-eight, and still with vigor and vitality, I soon realized that I must find more than a budget control and balance for my future to be secure. My time schedule of life in beautiful Hawaii was coming to an end. I left Hawaii in June 1993.

CHAPTER 25

SINGLE—NOW WHAT?

"Search me, O God, and know my heart,"
(Psalm 139:23).

With the Mililani Town condo in Hawaii sold, I realized that I no longer had any ties to the beautiful islands where I started a fabulous ministry with the military nineteen years earlier.

Moving for me seemed to be routine. However, this time the trauma was more painful. However, moving to Fishers, Indiana, was a very practical thing for me to do. I had just purchased a house there six months earlier. Virgie had chosen the location, and it was within one mile of the home of Duane and Sandy. I loved going to the place Virgie chose as our home, but now I am alone.

A New Path

Life for me has taken a different path. What I must do now is try to find purpose as a single man. I placed my trust in God to direct my future after the loss of my beautiful, loving, compassionate, and devoted companion of fifty years and eight months. We had enjoyed the pleasant times, endured the rough times, relied on the help of physicians, survived the times that implied finality of life, trusted in the dynamics of a knowing God, and recognized that life involves all of the above. After referring to the episodes of life with the above expressions, the present norm is a somber, uncertain episode of "now what"?

Adapting to life as a single person is not easy. I struggle to find happiness.

I begin to search for people who could help me. I did not have any interest in looking for another companion; I was just trying to take each day as an unknown part of my life's destiny.

I spent the first six months in Fishers, Indiana, trying to adjust to my single life. Since Duane and Sandy lived only a mile from the house, they were very helpful, but I was faced with a situation that mandated my attention. I had bought a condo in Daphne, Alabama, two years earlier by auction. My original purchase was made before the complex was even built. So now I had two condos in Alabama and a house in Indiana. A decision had to be made—where should I live?

At Christmastime, I decided to visit Ed and Letha in Daphne, Alabama. While there, I attended the Loxley Church of God where Brother James Cossey was pastor. The people were very friendly and kind, and I enjoyed the services. On New Year's Day, one of the church members who was a wonderful cook and hostess invited me, Ed, Letha, Ruby Slay, and three other ladies for dinner. When I sat down at the table, I noticed that five of the ladies there were widows. Laughing, I said to the hostess, "I think this is a set-up."

Instantly, Ruby said, "Wait just a minute—don't count me in that group you're thinking about." This created a laugh from all others. However, I had been told that one of the ladies was sure God had sent me to that area to be her husband.

A New Location

In July 1994, I decided to move to my condo in Daphne, Alabama. I helped Duane sell his house in Fishers and

I offered him and Sandy the house I had bought a year earlier. The arrangements for him taking my mortgage and not having to pay me an initial down payment permitted him a benefit.

Living in the beautiful condo in Daphne that overlooked Mobile Bay was an exciting experience. I had concluded this when I made the arrangements to buy this elegant property seven years earlier. With Ed and Letha living there also, I had the privilege of having meals with them often. Also, I understood they had a wonderful friendship with Ruby Slay who lived close by and also attended the Loxley Church. They had been close friends for nearly two years.

When I was in Greenville, South Carolina, as assistant pastor at Tremont Avenue Church, the Slay family served as senior pastors in 1953. Now I will have the closeness of a friendship that I had with the Slay family many years ago. Ruby and I would go on occasions to a local restaurant and have dinner. Since we were just good friends, we would alternately pay for these meals. Ruby had been a widow for over six years, and she reminded me that she was not interested in anything more than just friendship. To emphasize the reason for her strong stance, she showed me a ring on her finger and said, "Linwood gave me this wedding ring and I will never take it off."

New Friendships

In August I traveled to the General Assembly in San Antonio with Ed, Letha, and Ruby in Ed's van. It was a little unusual because some people who saw us traveling together presumed that Ruby and I were companions. Friendship was our position and nothing more.

My first experience reflecting a companionship other than friends after Virgie died, was initiated by my friend, Julian Robinson, at the General Assembly. Julian had lived in Chattanooga many years before, and knew a beautiful widow lady who was also at the General Assembly. He asked me if I would have lunch with her at the hotel sometime that week. He had known me and Virgie for many years. Knowing a friend, now a widow, he decided to become a match-maker. I was in a rather awkward position. To say the least—I was courteous. I had lunch with her one time but did not choose to follow up and see her again.

After the General Assembly, I was invited to speak at the Tremont Avenue Church for their 75th anniversary services. I decided to fly to Greenville, South Carolina, since I needed to make a fast trip. Two days after the Tremont event, the seniors had scheduled a trip to Branson, Missouri. I decided the trip to Branson would give me a good opportunity to get better acquainted with the people of the Loxley Church, since I planned to make that my church home.

I did not have an assigned seat on the bus, so I sat down by a lady I had seen at church. I asked if it was alright if I sat there. She said her husband would not like it if she was sitting by a man. So I got up. The only other seat available was beside a very attractive lady. She was very personable, a good conversationalist, and a widow. I learned she was not a member of the Church of God, but she enjoyed going on trips with their seniors. What I did not know at the time was that she was determined to have me as her husband. I had not had any inclinations to seek a companion since Virgie had passed on almost two years earlier. However, the more we talked and the more we were together, the more I realized that I was enjoying the company of this lovely lady, and she was enjoying every minute being in my company.

Complicating the twist of the story, I learned that Ruby was close friends with these two ladies on the bus, who are not so friendly with each other because they are both vying for my attention.

A New Page

When we arrived in Branson, one of the ladies cornered Ruby, asking her to intervene in the situation that seems to have me out of her reach. I found out later that both ladies were talking to Ruby about me. My week in Branson opened a page of my life where I was beginning to think about a companion. I found this attractive lady interesting. Because her husband had died the same week Virgie died, she thought this should be the key to opening our future companionship and ultimate marriage.

I had no feelings, other than friendship, with one of the ladies. The one I met on the bus was beginning to "pull at the strings of my heart" even though I had been told she had been married before. I learned later that she divorced him, married the second time, and then went back to her original spouse. This knowledge of the divorce and remarriage began to impact on doctrinal concepts I had believed all my spiritual life. I began to have extreme reservations about this friendship that seemed to be strong between us.

Ten days after returning home from Branson, a revival was beginning at our Loxley Church. A sermon, I believe to be God ordained toward me, was preached that Sunday night. The evangelist began his first words by saying: "God had changed my subject." Then he preached about

Ezekiel being admonished by God "to launch out into the deep." With this emphasis, he pinpointed the issue that so long as you are in shallow water, you are in control of all your actions within the shallow water. When you get into deep water—the current takes control. I became overwhelmed at the relativity of this message and the sensitivity I was feeling about a new companion. I immediately decided to break-up this developing relationship.

Sixty days went by after I broke all ties with the lady who believed I should be her next spouse. By this time I had a serious dialogue with Rudy as it related to how she should settle the conflicts between two of her best friends. That's when I became aware that we had a growing, glowing relationship—deeper than just friends.

A Deepening Friendship

During the week of the Lee University homecoming something happened between Ruby and me. When I called Ruby my first night away from Daphne, we had a wonderful telephone conversation. I was missing her and I think she was missing me. The next night, after the evening events at Lee concluded, I called her again. When I called, she answered, and I said, "Hello, Sweetheart." There was a long period of silence. When the conversation continued, Ruby seemed to be shocked but happy. We concluded our phone call with Ruby asking me if I would like to have lunch with her on the following day around 11:30 a.m. I assured her that I would be delighted. It was a seven-hour drive from Cleveland to Daphne, but I arrived on time.

During the next six weeks, everything was going like a speedy train. My time with Ruby was a special event.

She would have me over for lunch or dinner often. I would find that we had so much in common and our moods and thoughts were similar on whatever subject we discussed.

A New Condo

At the same time, I was involved in helping Ed complete the building of a new home in Loxley. He and Letha had decided a couple of months earlier to build. Letha had fallen and broken her ankle. Ed was continually in need of help because of his Parkinson's disease. Letha concluded that with both of them under a doctor's care, it was not wise for them to live on the twelfth floor of Loma Alta Towers. Their lovely home was finished quickly and they moved out of Daphne and into the town of Loxley as new residents. With this change in their residency, Ed negotiated with me to buy his twelfth-floor condo. I left the fifth floor and moved into my new quarters, feeling as though I was on top of the world. But now I owned three condos in Loma Alta Towers. I felt like a king because I had found a queen to soon become my companion.

A Lovely Sweetheart

Even though Ruby and I were "going together," we never sat together in church—Ruby's decision. So really no one knew of our relationship. But there is a first time for all things.

For the first time since finding a romance budding with my new sweetheart, I convinced Ruby to be seen with me publically. The seniors at church had their Thanksgiving dinner in the church gymnasium, a prominent meeting place for the church activities. I asked Ruby if I could take her.

She said, "You can take me, but we can't sit together."

"If I take you, I'm going to sit with you." I took her, and we sat together.

When we walked into the dining room, we sat opposite the pastor and his wife. The lady who believed I would be her companion looked at Ruby as she and I walked by her table. Only those who had known about the feeling between two lady friends on the senior's trip to Branson knew the situation now. I have such a feeling of ecstasy being with Ruby that I now can say publicly—I have a lovely sweetheart.

Ecstasy from Different Angles

I am now experiencing a mood that is so unusual. I have concluded that this longtime friend, Ruby, who I knew only remotely for so many years, has made a difference in my life. I have found a purpose for life and a reason for living.

While just sitting here, I thought about the past. I also anticipated the future. I felt like writing a poem to Ruby about both of these things—the past and the future. Below is that poem.

LIFE AND LOVE—12/01/1994

Today I recall some memories of happy days,
When youth and love came together,
Good times were mingled with hardship,
As love helped us live, work, and survive.

Thru heartaches and struggles we traveled.
Yet love made the bond more sublime,
The goals we set were before us,
As we labored together thru time.

My first love reached the end of her journey,
And she finished her living with joy.

The end of earth's toils she laid down,
On this very long day I recall.

Days and night since have been lonely,
As I remembered the love of my youth,
For fifty blest years she was sunshine,
As we labored and loved in the truth.

Two years have gone by since her passing,
As heavy were my sorrow and sadness,
My heartache and heartbeat in those times,
Bring memories reflecting our true love.

Virgie has finished her journey,
And today enjoys her bliss paradise,
Which she longed for and yearned for in love,
With Him who called from above.

My life has been affected by her passing,
As sadness and time took their toll,
But time is the healer of heartache,
And love still is balm for the soul.

Most recently the shadows departed,
As the sunshine of "your life" burst through.
From the life and the beauty of sunshine,
And I started loving anew.

That sunshine and beauty came thru Ruby,
As she shows me love comes from above,
As we talk and remember the old times,
When each of us reveled in love.

A new day, a new hope now blossoms,
Like the flowers that bud in the spring,
Life's winter with sorrow is ending,
"As love came to me in a swing."

The songbird sings and is happy,
As joy and peace make my journey,
A time to share, love, and to sing,
With my new love who is everything.

Dear Ruby, please share my affection,
And know how I feel as I sing,
That the flicker of love and living,
Has come through the joys which you bring.

Your ever loving—"Honey"
—Wayne.

CHAPTER 26

I MARRIED MY SWEETHEART

"It is not good that man should be alone"
(Genesis 1:18).

The moments that flew by was very difficult for me. I didn't have enough hours in the day to accomplish all of the things that I needed to do. I wanted everything to be precise. I found the lady I really loved who was far above the ordinary as far as I was concerned. Ruby Slay was so unusual that I began to review who she was and what she did that made her stand out so much higher than ladies with whom I had recent contact.

Remembering my last four months of activity with numerous people on the Branson trip, I have concluded that Ruby is far above those who vied for my attention. She excelled in beauty, elegance, attitude, intelligence, cordial personality, and so much more. In order to amplify the facts I am attempting to define, I will return to Ruby's earlier years. Then the story will unfold and it will be seen why I have made such quick action to capture this person as my future companion.

My Future Wife

Ruby was the spouse of one of the most famous people I had known in all of my ministry. He was none other than Dr. James Linwood Slay, "Prince of Preachers," as he was known by everyone who knew him. Ruby had excelled not only in her position as companion of Dr. Slay in his ministry but also because she had achieved recognition in the field of education.

The Slay family moved from Virginia to Cleveland, Tennessee, in 1962. Ruby taught in the Cleveland school system for five years. During this time, she was asked to serve on a committee to write the Title I program for Cleveland City Schools. The program contained four components: kindergarten, music classes, remedial reading, and a school nurse. These programs were to be implemented in the elementary schools that met the requirements of the government program.

Due to circumstances that developed, two of the committee members decided not to write their assigned part. Ruby was asked, and she agreed, to write the entire program. Upon completion, Ruby submitted the program to the Cleveland City School Board and superintendent. When the program was accepted, she was appointed by the Cleveland City School superintendent and board as Title I director.

Upon learning that schools who qualified for Title I funds had such an impressive program, parents began to question why the other Cleveland elementary schools could not have the same programs. The school board agreed to make them available. To do so, the school board had to assume full funding for kindergarten, music classes, remedial reading, and a school nurse for elementary schools. Future Title I programs were focused on other areas.

After Dr. Donald Yates came to Cleveland as the new superintendent, Ruby was asked to accept the position of supervisor of elementary schools, grades 1-6 in addition to Title I director. With the inclusion of kindergarten, elementary schools became grades K—6.

Ruby retired from her position when Linwood, due to his health, retired as professor at Lee College in 1978, and they moved to Alabama. Ruby returned to Cleveland in January 1979 at the request of Dr. Yates to serve as principal of Arnold School in Cleveland for the balance of the spring school term in 1979. They lived at the Holiday Inn for four months.

After completing the term as principal of Arnold School, Ruby and Linwood returned to their newly constructed retirement home in Daphne, Alabama. The home was in the Lake Forest subdivision. It was said to be the largest subdivision in any community in the state of Alabama. They were among the early occupants of the community with a prime location on a corner lot in the subdivision.

When I came back to my condo I had bought seven years earlier, I found this exquisite subdivision very close to the Loma Alta Towers complex. When everything in my whirlwind courtship so quickly revealed my ideals, I made a swift approach to Ruby.

Having posed my status as I defined it in the poem in the previous chapter, I now must find a way to convince Ruby of my love and do what I can to express rationale to influence this elegant lady. One evening when Ruby was visiting me at the condo, I gave a very calculated rendition of a reason why she should not only listen to my new proposal but also act on it.

I began my appeal for her response with the following: "If you will marry me, I will bring you to this elegant twelfth-floor penthouse overlooking Mobile Bay. Here you will see the most beautiful sunsets and blue waters of the Bay and you will have the best property as your home in this fabulous Towers complex."

Ruby responded so speedily that I lost all of my finesse. She said, "Yeah, but I can't grow flowers in concrete."

I realized very quickly that this was not good enough to tell me she was going to marry me for this—just declined—reason. My fast reaction was, "Okay then, I will move in with you when the time comes."

Ruby is a very exciting person. She has made me aware that out interests are more than mere friendships. The biggest problem lies in the issue of the difference in age between us. Linwood was four years older than Ruby. I come into this picture as one who is almost nine years younger. How will this work? It is a simple rule that an older person normally is the one in charge. To accept this rule would have me "as a puppet" when issues are to be rendered final.

To say that age doesn't enter into the issue is also too complex. To say that in spite of age each of us will treat the other equal, is the most probable option because love is not based on age.

Bellingrath Gardens

Just days after I suggested that Ruby make the penthouse her future home, I took her to Bellingrath Gardens on the southern outskirts of Mobile. This garden had become famous because of the method of keeping flowers on its premises blooming year round. Here on the river's edge, I made my appeal to her again.

There was a dock make of wood planks attached to floating units. At this large dock, small boats would come from nearby Mobile Bay. The river was serene because of its proximity to the wild growth nearby, as well as this famous garden. On the floor of this floating dock were tables and chairs for picnicking. Also, there were benches used for rest in case one was desired. It was here that I knelt at the feet of Ruby to make my next appeal. The proposal I created in poetic form is titled . . .

DEAREST RUBY—IT'S TIME

Time stood still the other day,
As you walked by,
Then I stopped to say, "I love you and I always will.
I love you now and I shall until."

The time will come if you'll agree,
To share my love, And our future be,
When we shall say our vows and I pledge to thee,
To love, thrill, and fulfill you,
And make you happy.

With the flicker of your charm and grace,
As I look into your smiling face,
Your words thrill me, Ruby, darling, dear.
They excite me as I hold you near.

Time has brought us down the path,
Of that beautiful garden called Bellingrath,
The place—the spot—where we shall bring,
Our love, our moods, into the swing.

Our time is now, when we shall be,
Fulfilled thru love—
And I shall ask you please,
As I've said my prayers to God for thee,
"Dearest Ruby, will you marry me?"

> The time is now—please by my queen,
> The date today—December 14,
> The time, the place, will you answer me?
>
> As I ask you Dear "My bride to be"
> The time has come; this is the place,
> As I look for and wait your embrace,
> As you give to me your sweet caress,
> Along with love, please answer yes.
>
> I'll be your man; please be my wife,
> I'll love and caress you for the rest of my life,
> If you will answer yes to bring us joy and bliss,
> Please answer now—sealed with a kiss.
>
> My time is your time—so that our time
> will be Forever—until"
> Maybe you'll never know how much I love you . . .
> But I'll keep looking for new ways to show you.
>
> Always—with love!
>
> —Wayne

It took me two times appealing my cause before this beautiful sweetheart gave me the answer I pleaded for that day. I think the shock of my using poetry again, shook her thinking *"what if—how—when."*

After a long time of embrace and excitement about this wonderful event, we left Bellingrath and went to Biloxi, Mississippi, for a celebration dinner. After dinner, a comment was registered about my seeking rings to finalize this event. Ruby had a previous contact with her granddaughter, Jessica, who worked for Service Merchandise Mart in Nashville. I think Ruby was about to believe that my proposal time was near. A special discount existed for a very short time for a purchase to receive that discount.

That firm had a location in Mobile. We drove to Mobile and bought engagement rings that night. Our decision to drive to Loxley to tell Ed and Letha about this wonderful special event made our day.

A Retired Minister

The church at Loxley was a great congregation. I was accepted into their fellowship and I was excited to be a retired preacher. I was one of the crowd who occupied the pew. It was pleasant to adapt with a fine fellowship. Ruby had been a member at Loxley since 1988 after the passing of Linwood. With her abilities in writing, Ruby created various comedy plays and skits for the seniors of the church. With my moving back south from Indiana in mid-year, I became a member and a participant in these efforts.

Five months passed from the date of my marriage proposal. Everything was being geared-up for our wedding day. The date was set, the program printed, and invitations were mailed. The difficult problem was how to send to only a certain few of the church people? To invite some and exclude others would be inexcusable. We, therefore, wrote a note in the Sunday bulletin that everybody was welcome.

Ed and Letha had finished their new home just months before our wedding schedule. They were arranging to celebrate their fiftieth wedding anniversary in two segments; one for the friends and family in Loxley on April 8, and one for the Texas clan on April 22. They told us that if we would help decorate the gazebo in the backyard for their celebration, we could have the 15th as our date. This was a splendid arrangement for both parties. We made all the arrangements for a lovely outdoor wedding.

All of our children's schedules fit into our schedule—Rusty, Dianne, and Jennifer; Jerry, Susan, Jason, and Jessica; Duane, Sandy Dawn, Daronda, and Darren—extended family, church attendants, and friends beyond description. A honeymoon cruise departing from New Orleans was arranged to take us to five different countries and islands. It was a beautiful one-week trip for one happy couple.

CHAPTER 27

MY FUTURE AT LOXLEY

"What is man, that thou are mindful of him"
(Psalm 8:4).

Before our marriage, Ruby and I began a wonderful time of adapting her house to accommodate me. Remember, she told me a few months earlier that she couldn't grow flowers in concrete. I had tried to influence her to move into my twelfth-floor penthouse after marrying me. Now the arrangement focused on enlarging the bath of the master bedroom. The house had a splendid three-bedroom layout. The master bedroom had a small bath. Ruby's design was to enlarge the area to include a new bath and closet area. The expansion was completed and new shingles were put on the whole house. The house had a new look because of our renovations and interior painting.

A New Ministry

Ruby had been very helpful in the local church. For seven years prior to my arrival in Loxley, she had worked with much dedication to help the previous pastor and wife, Luther and Rachel Quinley with drama programs. When James and Myrlene Cossey followed them, Ruby continued as a strong lay leader with local church ministries. After our marriage, it was proposed by Pastor Cossey that we become the leaders with a new assignment and title. We became pastor of the seniors in the church. It was a splendid opportunity to enlarge a new ministry. There were about 250 families on the mailing register who were classified as seniors. Because I had resigned my Honolulu church two years earlier and had lost a loving companion, I assumed that perhaps I would just fade away as far as ministry was concerned. After all, I was now 70 years old and it seemed to be the rule that ministers retired at eligibility time for Social Security. This was not to be. I got excited to find that I could become a serving, subordinate minister and help develop a strong department for seniors in a wonderful church. The pay was minimal because the church was not that strong financially to pay a full-time salary. Ruby and I were both drawing Social Security, so it was not imperative that we have a full salary.

Along with ministerial duties, Ruby continued to produce plays with the seniors acting in the productions. Most of her plays were comedy skits. One major purpose for producing these plays was to be able to sell tickets to a two- or three-night presentation. The seniors' primary objectives were to be able to take trips to places like Dollywood and Disneyworld. The productions would bring in more than $3,000 in ticket sales. Once a year, the seniors would enjoy fun and fellowship in some major place at a very modest price because of our yearly productions.

One year a schedule was set to take the seniors on a cruise to the islands of the Caribbean. This took a lot of effort and it was necessary to have them pay a supplemental portion. This type of effort made our senior program strong. We served for five years in this capacity.

Traveling the World

Though we served the seniors, we were not regulated as being employed full time, since we did not have pay for full-time service. Consequently, we had time to travel on our own. Most exciting was the fact that we could make our travel schedules anywhere we chose. Of primary interest were two- and three-week cruises. The longer cruises were so interesting because we could unpack the suitcase upon entering the ship and have daily sightseeing tours. Then after overnight sailing to the next port of interest, we would follow the same schedule each day. Ruby and I scheduled at least one cruise a year. One year, we made three cruises in a twelve-month period.

Many events stand out in memory. On the trip to the Mediterranean countries, our first stop was Greece. Seeing world famous locations in and near the city of Athens was exhilarating—particularly the Parthenon. To visit Ephesus in Asia Minor (now Turkey), made us feel as though we were there in the times of the apostle Paul. When we arrived in Damascus, we saw the locations that Saul of Tarsus (later known as Paul) notes in his travels according to the Book of Acts. At the Sea of Galilee, we saw the waters that Christ made famous.

At the Jordon River, water baptism ceremonies took place. At Jerusalem, we walked where Christ walked and prayed at the Temple Wall. At Bethlehem, we saw the location where the angels announced the birth of Jesus. Visiting the Dead Sea and the surrounding area of Jericho made our Holy Land trip so exciting.

When we went to Cairo and walked to the place of the Sphinx and the Pyramids, we felt as though we were in the historical times of Moses. To sail from Egypt to Italy and see the historical places of Rome, the Coliseum, and the Vatican made history unfold to us. Visiting the city of Tuscany and having lunch at the leaning Tower of Pisa was exciting.

That same fall we took a South American cruise. Traveling in waters with sixty foot waves around the Falkland Islands was difficult. Visiting the Straits of Magellan and stopping at the southernmost tip of South America in Chile, we took a walking trip to see a penguin rookery. What was dramatic about this segment of the trip was having to walk almost a mile in temperature near 32 degrees, but we made it to see the penguins. Ruby braved the cold winds and we saw hundreds of penguins. It was her 82nd birthday.

South Africa Trip

In 1999 Ruby and I took a trip to South Africa. Our first stop was in Amsterdam, Holland. We spent a day visiting many sights in this famous city. It was also a time for us to adjust to the six-hour time zone difference. We traveled across Europe, over the Mediterranean Sea, and then crossed the largest continent of the planet from north to south and landed in Johannesburg, South Africa.

Friends of Ruby, Pat and Yvonne van Niekerk, were our hosts for a thirty-day journey in South Africa to places Ruby and Linwood had known when they ministered there in 1952-1953. Other points of interest were put into our travel plans. The first week was spent in Kruger National Park. This is the famous animal sanctuary of wild animals of every kind. This 300-mile long park is controlled very securely for travelers' interest. The first animal I saw was a giraffe. I was so excited. I had seen many giraffes in zoos, but to see one in its own environment with his coloring was absolutely beautiful. My first thought was to jump out of the car and take a picture. However, due to the yelling of Ruby, Pat, and Yvonne, I quickly realized the danger and took my pictures from the car.

I wanted very much to see elephants. It took us seven days before we came to where they were. The problem was, at that time, there was a drought and the elephants were migrating south in search of water. When I saw the head of one in a ravine to my left, I yelled for Pat to stop for a picture. Pat assured me that the elephants would be seen in a few minutes. Sure enough, in less than five minutes we saw a herd of more than fifty mothers and babies cross our road. There were no male elephants in this group. However, I saw both males and females later in our travels. Lions, tigers, water buffalo, and many smaller animals filled our week while we were in their habitat.

Our travel by plane to Cape Town brought us to a famous area of South Africa. Table Mountain and other sites in that area are world famous. I decided I would cross the southern coast by car. The midpoint was Elizabethton, and from there to Durban on the southeast coast of South Africa. My difficulties surfaced immediately when I started driving. In South Africa, driving is on the left side of the road and the driver sits on the right side of the car. The cars have all mechanisms to follow these conditions. I believed I could do what must be done to become a driver on "the wrong side of the road."

In just a matter of moments after I entered the car, I sideswiped a mirror from a car at curbside in Cape Town. Ruby yelled, "Look out," but it was too late. Fortunately, the impact was only a contact of the two mirrors. There was no major damage. In Cape Town and Elizabethton, we purchased gifts from that country. After arriving in Durban, we traveled inland to Swaziland. This area was interesting because the Black culture of the natives of that area demonstrated their native costumes and did their dances.

At a local restaurant, we celebrated my birthday. The flowers of the area made a gorgeous background for photographs. I enjoyed sharing with our Durban pastor that I was 75 years old that day. When dialogue unfolded about Ruby's age, it seemed to be unusual to him that a man would marry someone older than he. I was asked to speak the next morning in the church service, Ruby was introduced prior to my sermon. He wanted to talk about the difference in our ages, but protocol wouldn't seem to allow it. Ruby got a good laugh from everyone when she said, "You don't think, at my age (79), I would marry someone older than I."

After returning to Pretoria and Johannesburg, we spent time shopping for African trinkets. Next, we flew to Victoria Falls in Zimbabwe. It was so unusual that again, my name was registered at the hotel as Wayne Hell—as it was twenty-five years earlier during my military assignment.

Lake Victoria is located in two countries, Zimbabwe and Zambia. The falls are world famous for being over 300 feet. We traveled from our hotel by car across the border of Zambia to view the lake. Then we took a helicopter to view the lake and falls. Two large groups of hippopotamuses were seen from the air. Africa is so distinct in its scenery. We spent the last days with our hosts in Magales Park in the Northern Cape of South Africa. Images of land and wild animals live on in my memory. I have traveled to five of the seven continents of the earth and every state in our nation. South Africa stands out as being nearly equal to the good old U.S.A, but nothing can "top" the United States of America from any angle of definition or description.

India and Southeast Asia

Because I had arranged this trip to use my air mile accumulation with Delta, all of the travel benefits were established at first class level on air fare, hotel, and ship travel. This trip was 35 days by air and sea. We left Los Angeles and arrived in India about thirty-two hours later. We spent two weeks sightseeing in many locations there.

Our first stop was New Delhi, the capital of India. We were placed in a five-star hotel at every stop on our journey throughout this thirty-five day trip. What was so devastating in Delhi was to see the poverty and slums that existed within this country. While we were staying in high-quality hotels, we saw the abject poverty of the nation.

By bus we went south toward the world famous Taj Mahal. Along the way we saw the style of life from every angle—women washed clothes in streams and put them on rocks to dry. Also, we saw women accumulating "cow pies" to be used for creating their fires for cooking of food. When we got to the Taj, the majesty of this funeral monument for one of India's queens could not be described.

From there, we flew to the west coast of India and saw the magnificence of the industry of Mumbai. We took a ship from Mumbai (Bombay in previous history) to the tip of India and then across the Indian ocean to Thailand. A stop to shop and purchase gifts made this place a notable place of memory. This was the same vicinity that the tsunami took its tragic toll some years later.

In Singapore we visited missionary friends. We traveled to Bali and viewed scenery and locations where Linwood Slay had visited when he was field director for the Missions Department thirty years earlier. We bought some art carvings similar to those Linwood had purchased when he was there.

From Bali we headed by ship through the South China Sea to Manila. Before our arrival, the captain excitedly informed us at the evening meal that we had escaped the pirates the night before. A number of days in the Philippines brought back vivid memories of the years spent in the military assignment passing through Manila to Clark Air Base.

Our final portion of this journey took us to Hong Kong. Christmas day brought a complex problem. We were located, of course, in a five-star hotel. However, meals were our responsibility. When we saw that Christmas dinner at the hotel was priced at $255 , Ruby and I took a bus and went a mile over to a spaghetti house for our Christmas meal. This was our last of ten cruise trips because the events of 9/11 began to indicate that travel anywhere in the world was precarious.

New Business Formula

In 2002 I began to settle down from world travel because of the fears of being trapped in a country where our safety might not be assured. I had sold my equity in my properties in Loma Alta Towers to different buyers. After marrying Ruby Slay in 1995, I did not feel it would be in my best interest to retain these properties because the monthly maintenance fees were excessive. In 2001 a special couple entered my business. They became friends and associates in later years.

Jim and Pat Copeland entered our story because of his business venture. They lived in South Carolina but were doing business in Houston, Texas. Jim was a Texan and

Pat was from Georgia. They had lived in Houston and were in business there before moving to South Carolina. Now they felt that if they could find a location halfway between the two places, it would expedite their travel time by living in the Mobile area.

In searching for a place in the newspaper, they came across my "for sale" ad. My fifth-floor condo had been sold, and for some time, I was holding the note for payment, but the owners were getting a divorce and they wanted out of the mortgage. I informed the couple that I would take back the property if they would give me a quit-claim deed. Here Jim and Pat come into the picture. In reviewing their financial statement, I decided to accept them as a new buyer of 503 Loma Alta Towers. In time I found them to be very cordial and honest people.

Jim was in the plastics business in a plant in Houston. Our friendship ultimately became a relationship of joining with Jim in a small way in his business in Houston. Having graduated from the University of Houston many years earlier, it was very easy to locate his business in this great city. When conversation revealed that I had family in Houston, our friendship bonds were quickly joined. Jim asked me to become a partner with him on a 50/50 basis. I happened to have a sizable reserve of cash from the sales of property. I accepted his proposal, but in short order I found that his technique for keeping records was too loose for my methods of operation. I reversed my partnership and became a financial support by way of factoring invoices. This provided him with my cash, and I received my return on my investment on a thirty-day basis.

W. J. Brokerage

This name was created to be able to establish business identification between James Copeland and me. The "W" stands for Wayne and "J" stands for James. It was not registered for any partnership purposes. I used this identity to do necessary business between Jim and me. The value of this action was in the fact that I only carried the invoice for a limited time. Generally speaking it was "Net—30." The rate charged for the period was normally 5 percent monthly. This was the first time in my business experience that I had known the method of finance on short-term transactions. Because the business volume was large and the monetary value was generally also in large amounts, the activity in my factoring these monthly invoices was highly profitable.

My association with Jim and Pat was a financial blessing. When "age catch-up" puts a degree of slow pace on how much I do, as to what I did for so many years, I thank the Good Lord that I have learned how to find strength to accomplish my objectives—in spite of my weaknesses.

Business with Jim has been under the name of Copeland Investments. I have kept records for Jim as well as invoicing all of his clients. This has given me experience in bookkeeping from a commercial angle that I had not known before. From this perspective, I also have learned much more about keeping good records.

My ability to control how much I would invest in these monthly factoring of invoices has kept my budget in control. I have not had to live by the credit-card method with excessive credit-card debt. I have believed that knowledge is imperative to understanding how things should be. I have also been excited to find that I did not have to spend money just to be happy. To live within one's means is always the ideal. I found that I could spend a limited amount of my time with my business association with Jim Copeland and still have time to enjoy life in whatever way God would open the door. For over eleven years, I have had an ongoing relationship with Jim and Pat. At this same time, I had church-related activities.

Again–Loxley

James Cossey had been pastor at Loxley for over eight years. When he left in 2001, new leadership took control. In the course of five years, three new leaders served Loxley. Not everything went as those leaders wished. After serving five years as pastor to the seniors, Ruby and I were relieved of that assignment. At the time for local business elections for the church council, I was elected to serve at that level. I remember well the various levels of service in church work. This experience of being on a local church council reminded me of my earliest ministry days.

What I am saying now is to reveal that the whole range of service begins at the lowest level, ascends to each level as authority prevails. Then, whenever the position and authority diminishes, the assignment is again at the lowest level. I was very pleased to find when leadership sought my advice during the time of a divided congregation that my knowledge was helpful. Having dealt with this kind of problem during my administrative tenure, I sensed the mood of the pastor and congregation when no one seemed to know what to do or how to deal with the divided congregation.

For a period of two years, these complications and the related issues regarding a church budget made issues very precarious. The local church income dropped almost

$30,000 a month. Being a part of the church council, each month we had to try to find answers about how to keep our church from getting into budget default. The pastor was sincerely thankful and continued to seek my wisdom relating to the critical budget problems.

Hall of Prophets

The status of one's position in church work is generally always expressed in terms of service rendered, positions achieved, and the time to accomplish it. When a resume` is submitted to pinpoint these references, it is often in the form of a manuscript or book. This method of defining my ministry has been done with this autobiography. I take occasion, now, to define this position from a little different angle.

The Church of God has in its organization an identity of a special group of ministers called "Hall of Prophets." This is a reference to a very distinct group of ministers.

The requirements for induction into the Hall of Prophets are as follows:

> Induction into the Hall of Prophets is reserved for those certified ministers whose service to Jesus Christ and the Church of God has been meritorious. The Gallery of Pentecost at the Pentecostal Theological Seminary is designed for the display of an appropriate plaque to preserve the memory of the selected ministers whose consecration and dedication to the church is worthy of emulation. The individual should be esteemed as a true prophet of God.
>
> The candidate must be either deceased or reached the age of 65 years and have contributed a major portion of his life to a full-time, significant ministry in the Church of God.

The candidate must be nominated by the president and approved by the Board of Directors.

An endowment scholarship fund of not less than $25,000 must be established in the Pentecostal Theological Seminary in the candidate's name.

The induction ceremony for me was November 3, 2005. The event was an experience that gave me a special feeling of gratitude and simultaneously a high state of recognition. Having begun my ministry in 1943 with a credential number 06531, I am one of more than 69,000 persons who have been ordain credentialed by the Church of God. Now, I have been chosen to be listed in the Hall of Prophets. At the time of this writing in 2012, there have been 87 persons inducted into the Hall of Prophets.

During the ceremony of induction, tributes were received from special people. From the executive level of the church, Paul. L. Walker gave me a special tribute. Colleagues, church leaders, friends, and family members participated in the ceremony and gave me tributes as well. They included Cecil B. Knight, Wallace J. Sibley, Steven Jack Land, Jerry McNabb, Benjamin Perez, Don Aultman, Winona Aultman, Ron Cason, Stan Holder, C. Duane Heil, Sandy Heil, and C. Dawn Williams.

Pomp and ceremony were shown by the way the seminary gave me their recognition. The auditorium was filled with friends who gave me personal expressions. The luncheon had more comments from friends and family.

Of special significance during the ceremony was the identity and reference to Ruby and me. Ruby has the distinction of being, during her life, the spouse of two inductees. James Linwood Slay, her first husband, was inducted seven years before me. Now to have Ruby at my side and have the declaration that "this dynamic couple still has the fervor and zeal to minister where the opportunity is presented" is of great significance. From the beginning of my ministry, I have lived "as a minister with a passion and zeal for service." Pomp and ceremony are over. If I am only history on a wall of recognition, so be it. I do not seek for further accolades. My only desire is to hear my Blessed Lord say, "Well done—my child."

100 De Witt Circle

This number has been prominent in more ways than being a mailing address. When Linwood and Ruby retired from their work in 1978, they came to Lake Forest subdivision to buy a lot and build a house for their retirement. For more than twenty-five years, this location was a landmark of the people of the community. Since Ruby was very much an outdoors person, she was often seen by passersby working in her rose garden. This beautiful scene was on the corner of the block, and it was viewed by motor traffic and any others doing their walking exercises.

When I came back into the community in 1994, Lake Forest was a thriving subdivision of more than 3,000 homes. When we married in 1995, the town of Daphne was already considered a fabulous retirement community. People from Mobile would find this area in Daphne the most desirable because it was "Eastern Shore," and this made the community the ideal.

I enjoyed living with the beauty of the neighborhood as my blessing. When Ruby said she could not grow flowers in concrete (1204 Loma Alta Towers), I knew my future of a happy life was to be in the wonderful environment of her extraordinary rose garden.

After eight years, comments were made about what might be the conditions of finalizing equities if death should necessitate dividing premarital assets. The whole theme of action was that premarital details prescribed that when Ruby passed on, I would have legal right to remain in her house for only six months, and then I must move out so that the house assets could be divided to her heirs. It was reviewed and we concluded that distribution of the equity of the house would benefit Ruby's children with a pretax distribution of the house equity.

In December of 2003, the negotiation was finalized, with consent of her children, and I bought the house. My intent was to pay multiple payments to accelerate the payoff. The mortgage was paid in full in forty-six months—May 2007. Ruby was able to distribute, tax free, her equity to Rusty and Jerry. With ownership of the beautiful parcel that had been home to Ruby for over a quarter century before I came along, and for an additional twelve years after our marriage, we are about to depart from Daphne and move to Tennessee. The beauty of this story of 100 De Witt Circle is that Jim and Pat Copeland bought our home.

One More Month

Getting things in order for a move was challenging. We knew that everything that had been accumulated over decades in the attic, in storage closets, in boxes, crates, and six rooms of accumulated furniture must be disposed of or sold. We were going to a place where our living quarters consisted of only 856 square feet of space in our new apartment.

The first action we took was to set up for the old-fashioned garage sale. With the help of neighbors and friends from the church, we began to put items in order. When it was final, we had three garage sales. The most complex part of this action was to decide what furniture to sell. During one garage sale, a special episode took place. Delora Pate, a very personal friend, came to our house, and after selecting a large amount of items, she said, "When I awoke this morning, the Lord told me to purchase $300 of your yard-sale items. I don't need any of these things. I'm just doing what He told me to do."

We were overwhelmed at her comments. When all our sales were completed and the costs of our truck were paid, we broke even on our costs of moving. Before we finished, we decided that certain quality items would be given as gifts to those friends who helped us. Wayne and Naomi Donaldson not only helped us during the thirty-day preparation, but they also became the drivers of our truck to bring us to Cleveland. We arrived at Garden Plaza on June 7, 2007.

CHAPTER 28

MOVING AGAIN!

*"O give thanks unto the Lord;
for He is good"* (Psalm 136:1).

In researching my past, I have lived in 49 different houses that I called *home*. I have resided in twelve states of the United States. I have traveled to all fifty states of our nation and have visited forty-five other countries of the world. I have set foot in 112 major cities of the world. Even though I have moved a great many times, moving has never been a traumatic experience for me. When I am asked the question, "Where was your most favorite place to live?" my answer has always been, "The last place."

Our "What-If" Rule

Having lived in Daphne, Alabama, for thirteen years, I now considered myself to be a happy Southerner. We loved living at #100 DeWitt Circle. We were retired and life was pleasant. In the course of time though, it became more difficult to maintain our fast pace.

We finally felt that the efforts of maintaining our daily routine were becoming harder each year. Perhaps age was catching up with us. Nevertheless, we made our decision in 2007 to move to Cleveland, Tennessee, based on what we called a "what-if" rule. What if one of us becomes incapacitated, what would the other one do to maintain our daily routine? We concluded that the probability of any drastic event or circumstance could become impossible for us to continue our present lifestyle.

My brother, Ed and his wife, Letha, moved to Cleveland a few years earlier to be near family. Ed's health was continuing to fail because of Parkinson's disease. They had found a new facility called *Garden Plaza*. It was developed for multiple use for people whose health problems needed special care. Ed and Letha moved into the facility in 2006. At the Christmas season, we came to visit them. When we saw the place was designed to accommodate independent living as well as assisted living care, we concluded that Garden Plaza would soon be our home.

Garden Plaza at Cleveland

Life Care Centers of America are headquartered in Cleveland, Tennessee. The five-story building called Garden Plaza was designed to accommodate over 150 people in both the independent and assisted living apartments. The owner of the building determined to make the facility a "five-star class" facility. The accommodations were designed to meet the needs of residents.

The first requirement for occupancy was age—sixty five years or older. When we occupied apartment #512, the building was a year old. Our apartment was facing north at the front of the building. Traffic was seen on Keith Street moving north and south. Our apartment had a balcony so we had a pleasant view.

Esmerelda Lee, the general manager at Garden Plaza, had been an employee for a number of years with Life Care of America. When the new building called Garden Plaza opened, Esmeralda was selected as manager. Her efficiency as well as her personality keeps things moving well for the facility as well as for the occupants.

Living in our fifth-floor unit was comfortable. The area of our apartment was under 900 square feet. In addition to a beautiful apartment, we were provided two meals in the dining room daily, as well as many other accommodations and activities designed to make our social life pleasant.

Our lifestyle here is, in many ways, similar to that in Alabama. We had wonderful neighbors in Daphne and many church friends in Loxley and Mobile, Alabama. In Cleveland, our church family is the North Cleveland Church. This same church had been home to the Slay family when they were pastors of the church in the 1940 decade. Also, from 1962 to 1978, this congregation was known as their church family.

CHAPTER 29

HEALTH PROBLEMS

"Heal me, O Lord, and I shall be healed"
(Jeremiah 17:14).

Health insurance is very important for me. Ever since I had my first evidence of cancer, I have tried to keep a close review on my health. Ruby had good benefits through her school retirement plan. I was always searching for a secure position because my cancer problems were requiring close attention to my health needs. I had melanoma cancer in 1978, my first colon cancer in 1986, bladder and prostate cancer simultaneously in 1997. I was informed by my specialist that dermal cell skin cancer was my next problem, then squamous cell cancer. I entered the 2000 decade wondering how to be protected with health insurance.

I had problems continuously with my health insurance plan. Moving from Alabama to Tennessee did not give me the same benefits. The Tennessee plan was not as comprehensive as the plan I had subscribed to in Alabama. I was able to change companies with the help of Julian Robinson at headquarters. He identified Mutual of Omaha as being a more competent company than the one I was using. It took me six weeks before my acceptance was approved.

Bad News

With the move to Tennessee in 2007, I had failed to keep up with my schedule for my colon review. I had not had a colonoscopy in over five years. When I made the schedule to see a gastroenterologist, Dr. Paul Brundage, the report he gave and the pictures he showed of my ascending colon were grotesque and the report was that I had stage three colon cancer. The comments of my doctor was to find a surgeon immediately.

Good News

Because of congestive heart failure, I scheduled an appointment with my cardiologist, Steven Austin, in Chattanooga, who had been seeing me for the last two years. I needed to be sure my heart could take the stress of surgery. After reviewing my heart status, he confirmed that my heart was strong enough to sustain my needed colon surgery. His contacts with other doctors and surgeons led me to accept Dr. Marco Chavarria as my general surgeon. Dr. Larry Schlabach became my oncologist.

On January 1, 2009, my schedule was fixed. I had reapplied for Medicare and was now back under the Medicare program. I requested of Dr. Chavarria that whatever he must do, I wanted the surgery to be completed by connecting the remaining colon to my colostomy. I was advised that most likely I would have an ileostomy as my final state of surgical action. However, when it was over, my surgeon said, "We did it like you wanted; however, you only have one foot of colon remaining.

A Turn in the Road

Three days after my surgery, I had a heart failure problem. At 2 a. m. my heart rate went to 39. I was sent to emergency that morning for another surgery. This time the cardiology surgeon, Dr. Gbadebo, placed a congestive heart failure pacemaker with defibrillator in my chest.

When I reviewed the medical bill submitted to Medicare for my implant, it was priced at $60,000. Wow!

Diagnosis

One month after my dismissal from this traumatic experience, I went back to see Dr. Schlabach. He informed me that I still had some cancer cells in my body. When I asked him what his prognosis would be, he stated that if I did nothing I might live perhaps five years, but if I would take the chemo treatment he was suggesting, more than likely I could live longer. My immediate answer was. "Doctor, you do everything you propose and I will accept it, and the rest I will leave to God."

The plan called for me to take chemo pills as prescribed. After two months, I found the severity of the chemotherapy almost unbearable. I suffered loss of appetite and a skin rash that was giving me pain I could not tolerate. My doctor reduced the number of pills and I survived the six-months treatment.

Sepsis

Due to the results of the function of my digestive system, I had very grave problems when a stoma leak contaminates my bladder function. Three times I have had the microorganisms enter my blood system, and in less than twenty-four hours, the poison known as sepsis (blood poisoning) almost took my life. Again, a speedy trip to the emergency room of the hospital and the care of those who know my problems, with God's help, have brought me back to my normal routine.

Praise Be to God

One month after my chemo treatments, blood work was taken to review my status and found that I was cancer free. I have gone over three and a half years since my chemo treatment. I dramatically declare that the God who called me, is the same God, who with the medical procedure and doctor's care, has given me these times free of cancer. To God be the glory! Due to the results of these events, I took fifty pounds of weight from my body. This excited me because I am now able to breathe at night without the use of my c-pap machine, which I had been using for the last five years.

Vascular and Other Difficulties

Ruby has had problems relating to her blood system also. More than three years ago, a doctor told her the arteries in her legs were occluded (blocking blood flow). Two of the three arteries below the knee were totally blocked. The third artery was 90 percent blocked. Medically, nothing can be done. When the pain becomes unbearable, the only option will be amputation. With only ten percent of blood flow to her right leg and being diabetic, an ulcer developed on her right foot. It became a major issue for her life nineteen months ago.

The doctor who analyzed her problems recommended that she go to the "Wound Center" at the hospital to treat the ulcer under their care. Ruby would not accept that decision. She went to Esmerelda Lee for advice. Esmerelda called the nurse and director of physical therapy to her office to look at Ruby's very swollen, red foot and the ulcer. They agreed the situation did not look good. Finally, the physical director offered a suggestion. There was a procedure they might be able to do with the approval of a doctor. However, he certainly could not guarantee it would work. They would try it if we wanted them to. We agreed to the procedure, praying that it would keep Ruby from losing her foot to amputation.

Her primary care doctor authorized the procedure to be provided by the Physical Therapy Department of Garden Plaza. Due to the wonderful care of the physical therapists, her ulcer was completely healed. During the time of the infection, she was also treated with an antibiotic. After the first round of antibiotics, a stronger antibiotic was administered. This time it was too much. While the antibiotic did help the ulcerated flesh to find healing, through the therapy program another problem occurred. It was diagnosed as C-Dif. (a malfunction within the colon). All the good bacteria in the colon was destroyed because of the excessive strength of the second antibiotic. Ruby began to suffer colon problems and blood loss. It took seven months of care and much help from the medical field to bring this issue to a solution.

After the loss of 25 percent of her blood, a transfusion was given the first week of July 2011. God brought Ruby through severe pain because of the problems with her legs and the addition of C-Dif. The alternative help for Ruby's digestive problems is that she now takes a pro-biotic each day. While we endure our aches and pain together relating to our health problems, we rejoice in the Lord that He, who foreknows and knows all our situations and circumstances has brought us this far.

Yes—Moving Again

A notice had appeared that the corporate offices were announcing a new rental price for the recently completed patio homes adjacent to the Garden Plaza complex. The arrangements were available to anyone. I appealed to the realtor agent to see if we would be allowed to move. *Yes* was the answer. I convinced Ruby on Tuesday that she and I could complete our move with limited help.

During this same time of Ruby's therapy treatments, the event took place that brought both of us again to the brink of disaster. This was a real mistake and we paid dearly for it (she was 95 and I was 86). She packed boxes and I transported them by the two-wheel and four-wheel carts. Ruby unloaded the boxes and set everything in place. Special help from the Plaza team helped us with the heavy furniture. In three days we were "at home" in our patio home. It was 50 percent larger and the space made us feel that we were in a new state of elegance. However, in 48 hours, my heavy overwork in moving caused my stoma problems to contaminate my system. By Saturday night at eight o'clock, I was delirious. I was taken by ambulance to the hospital again with sepsis (blood poison of the blood stream).

Not knowing Ruby and I had moved, unpacked and had everything in place, Jerry and Susan came from Nolensville to help us get things in order. They stayed four hours with me in the emergency room. At midnight, they came back to the patio home. Ruby was too weak to visit me. Jerry stayed with her for a week. The following Sunday, she went to the hospital. Both of us barely survived the event of becoming new residents at # 24 Patio Homes, but thank God we did! Our journey together has been very adventurous and very wonderful. We both discovered that even though our first marriages were wonderful, we could fall in love again.

CHAPTER 30

SPECIAL TIMES

*"To every thing there is a season,
and a time to every purpose under the heaven"*
(Ecclesiastes 3:1).

Life for us is wonderful, in spite of the problems we now face relating to our age. We have had the pleasure of having friends visit us and do not feel any constraint by tight constricted quarters. We take life one day at a time—naturally! However, our pace is now much slower and much more cautious.

Though we have breakfast provided in the dining room, most of the time we opt to fix our first meal of the day in our kitchen. This does not compel us to fit into the 7 to 9 a.m. breakfast schedule mandated by Garden Plaza. It is also much more pleasant to have the meal we prepare to suit us. We often have our first meal closer to the lunch hour, so we then can call it *brunch*.

Birthday–Number 96

About three months prior to the event, I contacted the team at Garden Plaza to plan for a special birthday celebration for Ruby's 96th birthday. Ruby was reluctant to accept this kind of event in her behalf. I persisted because I said to her, "You only have one 96th birthday." I did not dictate how the staff was to prepare for the event. The only mandate I made was that the tables where the guests sat must have table cloths. I requested that the party be held in the atrium rather than the dining room. The atrium size would only accommodate seventy-five people after the center section of the food tables were allocated. Since birthdays of all the residents are recognized monthly at Garden Plaza, I had to use a very diplomatic process with this event.

Typically, the monthly recognized parties have almost everyone invited to attend. So I had to make this a party by invitation only. Knowing that not everyone who is invited will have their time schedule to fit to my proposed date, I had to presume on these conditions. I created a special letter identifying the reasons for the event and sent invitations to 100 people. The RSVP timetable for response allowed me the uncertain option of hoping everyone who wanted to come would be able to fit into this limited room. The total response was seventy-five people, just exactly the spaces provided by the plan.

The elegance of the food and fruit preparation was too beautiful to describe. The chefs had taken the directives from the top authority to make this party "top rate." The only thing I directed to Esmerelda was that I would pay the price to make this party the best. The price was set and I paid for it in advance.

The glamour was in the extravagance of the fruit presentation. At the front food table the chef sculpted a watermelon designed as a flower. At the center table was a special rose presentation. At each corner were three glass vases with red roses. The unusual drama of this presentation was that the roses were sculpted from strawberries. The birthday cake on the next table made the presentation complete. Of course, not everyone was there at the start of the event. This allowed Ruby to not only greet the people as they entered, but also go to their table after they had eaten their sandwiches and fruit, and then they reveled in this wonderful event. Comments by local residents said this party to be the most elegant they had seen in the six years birthday parties had been given.

General Assembly 2012

Attending a General Assembly is considered the primary event of one's year when you are in ministry in the church. I began my attendance to my first General Assembly in 1947. Ruby had been attending them every two years since she was a teenager. I missed only one General Assembly during my ministry in 1954 and that was when I was in Haiti in mission work and the mission budget did not provide for me to come. I have attended the General Assembly thirty-three times. Ruby has missed only two since she started attending in 1930. Her total is forty-nine.

Why do numbers matter? Perhaps they don't. But when church affairs, business rules, new laws, and elections of new leaders are the purpose of the General Assembly, this event is a drama that unfolds to each of us.

There is another reason for me to place emphasis here. Even though our desires were to attend, Ruby had concluded that the severe difficulties we encountered in traveling back and forth from the hotel to the convention for all the sessions during the last General Assembly would be impossible this year. For us to be able to survive the long walks for the 2012 General Assembly, an alternate method must be taken. Provisions were made for us to use two motorized scooters. We were blessed. Each night the scooters were charged electrically. The battery kept us mobile until the charge time came at the end of the day.

We each came home feeling that in spite of age, we had been able to do what could not have been done, if we had not had the scooters.

My Sibling's Timetable

About destiny, the wise writer in Scripture said dramatically: "A time to be born, and a time to die." Speaking of family brings me to pinpoint life from a different perspective. My family is listed in many places within this writing. What none of us knows is the time period of each of our lives. I had nine siblings who made my family a wonderful part of my life. Being the oldest, I was married at age seventeen when my youngest sibling was only one year old. The lives of each member of my family intertwined with mine over the years.

My brother A. C. (Punk) was a close person to me as it relates to attitude, personal success, and that which made him a strong business person. He helped me to sell property and became one of my choice brothers. Punk died from a colon surgery irregularity on July 4, 2002. He was the first to pass on. My brother David was next to the youngest, and two years later he died of stomach cancer. My sister, Wanda, was number six of the clan. She passed away in 2006. A time period of five years brought the calendar to 2011. My third brother, Ed, who had struggled with Parkinson's disease crossed into Paradise on April 11. My fourth brother, Darvel, passed away in October 2011. My sixth brother, Dean, went through five months of coma after his carotid artery surgery before he died in February of 2012.

While these references seem to dwell on the morbid, I rejoice to inform any reader, that having grown up in a very devout Christian family, everyone confessed Christ as Savior. There are only four of us left of Dad and Mom's children. No one knows the "when" timetable of each life, but I can assure you that God knows, and He will keep us in His care and in His timetable of life.

CHAPTER 31

LIFE'S COMPLEXITIES—
MY SYNOPSIS

*"And we know, that all things work together
for good to them that love God"*
(Romans 8:28).

I started the introduction of my autobiography with a quotation from an unknown source: "Life is but a dream." I followed that sentence by declaring, "Life is a reality." Having traveled life's journey for more than eighty-seven years, I declare with emphasis that my life has been more than a dream. Life's events have come from the activities I have encountered and time has revealed a complex life. These conditions are shown in the previous chapters to reveal each aspect of a problem or a conclusion to a complicated event of my life's story.

The best way to reflect on the good side of life is to reveal the events that made it so. The complex problems that affect the "hoped for good results" must be noted in order to define the good against the bad. It becomes necessary to reflect on all the facts so nothing is left out. The conclusion of a story or a plot in my life that was meant for good may not seem so in the final analysis. This is why I have used the term *complexity* in my writing.

To those who delve into the substance of my story, just remember that whenever the plot gets so complex, just keep reading. You will find, as I have, that God who knows every story's beginning also knows the end of the plot. It is with this emphasis that I declare that my God has helped me through the extreme parameters in my life. I have found that an event that seemed to affect me during the crisis time in which I encountered it was not the final solution. To this point I will reflect in a concise way to give a synopsis of my life's journey.

While I have reflected on every aspect of my journey, I emphasize that from the beginning, the God who directed me to minister to others is the priority of my life. But God, who foreknew the whole story plot has helped me through the bad and ugly aspects and brought me to the end of my life in a happy and joyful state.

Who Am I?

According to the official records of the Church of God Business and Records Department, I am known by my credentials as # 06531. After that, Wayne W. Heil is revealed as a person born November 15, 1924. Seventy years of my life as a preacher of the Gospel of Jesus Christ, I have served under the jurisdiction of the church. I received my call from God during a dedication service at a Bible School in Lemon, South Dakota, as an eleven-year-old boy. Five years later, at seventeen, preaching in Houston, Texas, I began a life of service to God, the church, the saved and the unsaved.

I was first credentialed on March 2, 1943. Bishop ordination was given May 3, 1955. My ministry has permitted me to serve in eighteen states during my stateside ministry and ministering worldwide in sixty-two countries. Other statistics show twenty-four churches organized; 4,462 sermons preached; 727 converted/restored; 336 sanctified;

308 baptized with the Holy Ghost; 680 baptized in water and 867 members added to the church.

In this wonderful life, I first began my service to God as a faithful member of the church. I became a Sunday school teacher as a teenager. In education achievement I received a Bachelor of Science degree, a Master of Arts and an honorary Doctor of Divinity degree. I served as church councilor, evangelist, pastor, state youth director, state evangelism director, missionary, Far East director of Ministry to the Military, state overseer, and as a member on many boards. While I do not intend now to give a full resume` of what I have done, I have chosen, by the preceding chapters, to write a complete story of my life.

Some Complexities

The first decade in my ministry was complex. In 1942 I decided to pursue my call to ministry by enrolling in B. T. S. on a split-moment decision. War was intensely affecting my life. As a student, marriage as a teenager, and working on government military bases, was critically affected when the school president informed me on a cold December day at the end of the first semester that I was financially broke, could not pay my tuition for the next semester, my wife was pregnant, and I "would not make it" regardless, so I must leave B. T. S. (Bible Training School) immediately.

In spite of the edict to leave my residency in the dormitory, I found help from my professor, my friends, and my family to respond to many alternatives. I finished that term and graduated from B. T. S. the next year with honors. I began to realize that people can affect your life's ambition if you subscribe to everything which is alternatively presented. Though I was an eighth grade school drop-out without a diploma, I successfully achieved a college education with degrees.

My success as a builder, contractor, and engineer gave me an open door to many assignments in my church work. When asked by many how could I achieve my status so swiftly, I gave a simple answer to the inquisitive questioner, "They paid me as a minister and got me as a builder at no extra cost."

My success and achievements in my first twenty years were gratifying. Others seemed to question how or why my assignments should reward me with continued excellent appointments and status. All this came to a devastating calamity when my "God-motivated response" to a congregation called for my eviction as their leader.

During the Civil Rights Era in the 1960 decade, I responded to one of my local church councils that I had no restraint in having Blacks worshiping with us. If God could forgive any nation or person regardless of color, so would I. Having served as a leader for three years in Haiti where everyone was black but me, I certainly felt compelled to allow the same color in our service. Church policy did not mandate that the black people could not come in, but the people of Mississippi were at the center of this nationwide boiling pot of racism. Consequently, I did not survive the issue.

The question is posed. Is this church politics? In the 1960 decade, it was totally incomprehensible for any church leader to think this kind of church function could prevail. Today, church polity, policy, and politics opened every door to all colors and nationalities. I know Pastor Dwight E Allen of a Church of God congregation in the

Miami area where over fifty different nationalities worship together today.

Religious Zig and Zag

When is it proper to declare whether one is conservative or liberal. It depends where you are when the question is posed. If you are involved within a group that is totally opposite your political views, you would be classified as anti to that policy.

The Church of God has had an extreme variation in its ethical concepts since its organization. In the first four decades of the last century, the concepts of the church body, as ratified by the ordained ministers, were expressly negatively directed. From the beginning, the organization dogma has been radically ultra conservative. At the midcentury, the dogma became a little less dogmatic and quite a bit more liberal. In the last three decades, the liberal dogma seems to imply "Don't rock the boat."

From the standpoint of analyzing the synthesis of the church, in 1982 I took time to review the philosophy of the church government, its polity, legal ethics, procedures, and ultimate conclusions that were reached because of decisions that were rendered relevant to the church. Most of the issues that are reviewed are defined by church authority as "change." I wrote a master's thesis relating these issues. Because I had come through a very severe time while I was the senior authority in charge of my jurisdiction (State Overseer of New Jersey), I determined there was a necessity to defend the church from every aspect within my jurisdiction at that time. I was compelled, seven times in eight months, by the issues to go to civil court to defend the constitutionality of our church law relating to church polity.

A conclusion relating to the emphasis I relate hereto has to do with legal interpretation. When a person attempts to violate the legal precepts under which he has delegated himself, everything gets into disarray. From these issues, I coined an axiom that became a part of my legal thesis. I post it in this writing for review and scrutiny.

>If authority is *mis*used,
>And polity or law is *mis*applied,
>Then justice has been *mis*appropriated,
>And judgment is a mistake.

What seems so difficult for religion scholars to reckon with has to do with areas that overlap from the civil law to religious law and those with whom the conditions intertwine. In the civil realm, we smear those who are guilty of violating logical conclusions in their actions. In this light, we brand them as bad politicians. For every polity, there is a policy, and every policy delves into politics. And with politics we brand politicians. Similarly, in the church realm, we must have church polity. With polity must come policy. Also with policy comes politics. But we do not wish to classify ministers as politicians. While it seems drastic to brand church leaders as bad, sometimes they are convicted of violating church law.

No person, civil or religious, is immune from compliance with the law, whether the civil law or the law of God. I have accepted these principals for my life. They have been the force that gave me my sense of direction. Submitting my life to God as a young boy, I have determined that I shall be controlled by those rules. I am first and foremost a minister.

When a person lives under our church law, the time factors regulating assignments are mandatory. Since I was chosen many times by my superiors to enter into different fields of ministry, I was not jeopardized by certain controls. The one thing that always affects the issue is age. Age becomes a factor and certain regulations relating to appointments entered into my equation.

Forty-two years of exciting ministry brought me to age 64. Most ministers try to believe that they must hurry to the next year to obtain Social Security with its benefits. Concurrently, this is the time most churches look for the younger, zealous, more vibrant leaders. To be able to retire with forty years of service does not necessarily become a tried-and-proven reality. I had worked half of these forty years attempting to secure a stable financial status by retirement time. Now I have concurrently accomplished my goals along these lines.

The next three years put me into a tailspin. The saving and loan system collapse during this time affected me also with a financial collapse. In three years I had to absorb $1 million loss in net worth. At this same time, I had my second cancer surgery and was informed by my medical advisors to find some place to enjoy my last days. A third event from my church authorities alleged a fiduciary question during my last state appointment. It took two years of time and reams of paperwork (which I had from my files to certify my integrity in all the actions) to validate my innocence and certify the validity of my position within my authority jurisdiction. This number of issues in my life help to show me that the zig-zag of these times placed me at the altar of "why me, Lord"? I did not believe within my personal philosophy that because I had reached retirement age, as some suppose, that I must call it quits.

After making a valiant recovery in health, I began a new era of life. I served God and the church six more years in Hawaii. Twelve years of ministry in Alabama brought me to the moment to define my status in my ministry as retired.

More exciting is my reflection on the special time I have had to reflect on my new love life. For more than seventeen years Ruby and I have had the most excellent time of living life to the fullest. After the loss of each spouse, and with that half-century of history permanently sealed in God's Treasure of Memories, we have shared in ministry —together; enjoyed normal life routine—together; traveled the world—together, and have come to enjoy a retirement lifestyle together. For the last five years, Garden Plaza has been home.

Because God was knowledgeable of all the issues that I have referred to in this story of my life, and because I came to know that God cared for me, I traveled a complex chart along my life's journey. BUT GOD who knew the problems before they happened, and knew the solutions when they came, brought me this far by faith. God's provisions, financially, materially, and the aesthetics of a beautiful life with a loving companion have made it possible for us to live life "to the fullest" without financial worries because my God brought us through complexities along my life's journey—BUT GOD is still in control.

I am still enjoying life. How much longer though, only God knows. But the moment expressed by Robert E. Selle in his dramatic conclusion of mortality, will finalize my story dramatically.

Think of stepping on shore
And finding it heaven!
Of taking hold of a hand
And finding it God's hand!

Of breathing new air
And finding it celestial!

Of feeling invigorated
And finding it immortality!

Of passing from storm and tempest
To an unbroken calm;

Of waking and finding yourself HOME!

—Robert E. Selle